A DICTIONARY OF
MEDIA TERMS

EDMUND PENNEY

G. P. PUTNAM'S SONS
New York

To Mercedes,
who cared and believed

Library of Congress Cataloging in Publication Data

Penney, Edmund.
A dictionary of media terms.

Bibliography: p.
1. Mass media—Dictionaries.   I. Title.
P87.5.P4   1984   001.51′03′21   83–27051
ISBN 0–399–12958–8

Printed in the United States of America

ACKNOWLEDGMENTS

My special gratitude to Grant Loucks of Alan Gordon Enterprises in Hollywood, for making special catalogues and glossaries available to me, and to the Academy of Motion Picture Arts and Sciences in general, and their staff in particular—Rose Arnold, Elaine Richard and Executive Director James Roberts.

In mentioning the Academy, I would also like to thank Norman Corwin, formerly head of the Documentary Film Committee at AMPAS, and now a member of the Board of Governors, for his excellent essay on documentary film. It is part of his new book, *Trivializing America*. Mrs. Alan Stensvold has been most gracious in allowing me to reprint the Alan Stensvold film conversion footage/time chart, a standard work tool for cameramen, editors and directors.

I would like to comment upon the great amount of information I have absorbed from cameramen who have worked with me and whose brains I have cavalierly picked—Fred Hudson, Frank Johnson, Sven Walnum and others.

A hearty nod of appreciation is certainly due to the Disney bunch that I worked with—Randy Bright, Don Henderson, David Michener, Stormy Palmer, Kevin Reem and other Mousketeers and Imagineers.

Then too, there are the lab folk at HFE and CFI—Sid Solo, Mickey Kaplan, Bob Ward, Seymour, Wally and Marvin. My acknowledgments to them for putting me straight over the years as to my initial and total misconceptions of lab practices and terminology.

From Gerson and Gertrude Marks, and David Kitsis, I learned much about the legal aspects of the media business in general, and about production contractual procedure in particular.

From producers and distributors such as Irwin Braun, Dave Adams and Jim Ganzer I was given insights and help over the years, and they certainly extended my technical vocabulary in relation to production and distribution.

There are the random names of those who gave input to this dictionary, knowingly or not: editors Lisa Day, Bob Fisher, Gene Fowler, Noelle Imparato, Ron Peterson; sound technicians Irv Naf-

3

shun, Steve Speidel and Jay Wertz; directors Ed Beatty, Jack Daniels, Cecil B. de Mille, Albert McCleery, Gerald Schnitzer, Orson Welles; writers and journalists Syd Cassyd, Frank Orme and members of the Hollywood Foreign Press; also True Boardman, Anthony Cardoza, Bill Cartwright, John Daniel, Stewart Engebretson, Tom Jozwiak, Frank Leonetti, Barry Scharf, Brant Sloan and David Wiley.

Further, there are those multitudes of grips, technicians, actors, production managers, drivers and other media people on both sides of the camera whose repeated usage of the trade vocabulary finally managed to impinge itself upon my consciousness. Two immediately come to mind: grip Don Capel and transportation captain Danny Delgado.

Finally, to my drama teachers from grammar school and junior high school days who opened up this whole wonderful world of professional make-believe to me, my deepest thanks. They were Nelle C. Wiley and Ola Fern Walker.

To all of them, may this dictionary reflect the high level and professional excellence of their assistance.

CONTENTS

INTRODUCTION

THE BIG STUFF OF SMALL TALK

I have been around, we have all been around, language, lingo, slang, euphemism, jargon, pow-wow sign talk, most of our lives. Yet how rarely do we stop and stare, parse and ponder, the incredible words that leap out of our mouths to slide in other people's ears to make popcorn ideas inside their heads.

That the study of linguistics as fun and games, not stuffy research, is not central to this playground we call life, has always stumped me. The love of words, acrobats all, tumbling in from around the world, seems natural to me and my wife.

Maggie tutors technical French at the University of Southern California.

Technical French? people gasp. What in blazes is *that?*

They gasp, of course, without stopping to think. For if you pause one moment you realize, as my wife points out, that when you step into your garage repair shop you immediately begin to speak machinists' English. At the hardware store, the dealer vocalizes in device gibberish: gimcracks, doohingies and whatchamacallits. At your druggist's? Does or does not your pharmacist chat and write in pharmaceutical English or Latin laboratory combinations thereof? Lunch with a sociologist and he will fall into his sibling mumbo-jumbo during the first beer. Dine with your least-favorite psychiatrist and he'll palaver forth Freudian subjunctives. Grab the *Wall Street Journal*: all Greek.

In sum, we are surrounded, no, drowned in so many sorts of technical language each day that we cease to notice.

It follows that many of these various clans of ideas rarely cross-pollinate or even try to understand each other's bushwah, bombast, or the merest noun having to do with psychopaths, washernuts, accident prones, Dow Jones averages or recombinant DNA.

Resultantly, the shelves of libraries and bookstores have begun to yeast with new and yet newer brands of *linguine,* as one Italian devourer of words once put it.

The Industrial Revolution of just yesterday reshaped not only society, but its mind and tongue. The electronic and computer revolutions are doing the same. Tagging along with all this we find a tad that only began to speak some sixty years ago, motion pictures, and their bastard brother TV, both with their attendant and mysterious devices.

This is a book about, then, about that new lingo that grew up with film hardware, hard and soft, and sprouted into and through the at first unwanted child Video.

Here in this Curiosity Shop you will find words that simply did not exist 80 years ago, or which have been refurbished for new use in mid-century. Many of the alien nouns here have only come into play within the last twenty years.

It follows that, prowling through this mechanical display bin of language, one is as fascinated as one can be with any dictionary, anywhere, anytime. For if we are not fascinated with the words that surprise our epiglottis or are printed out to delight our eyes, what *is* there in the world to be fascinated by?

Words are, after all, what we are completely and soully about, since we are the only true mind-beasts that inhabit our amazing planet.

Well, enough of kicking the dead horse alive. Here is the talk, here are the words that encompass the ideas that lubricate an Industry to help make of it an Art.

Jump in. But be careful not to trip over the clapper board, the Green-Man, or the Release Negative.

Here—let *me* go first.

RAY BRADBURY
Los Angeles, California

FOREWORD

It says something essential about the Gypsy-camp cultural isolation of the people in show business—"showbiz" as *Variety* calls it—that we refer to all mass media in general as *"the* business." What a broad, sweeping term that is. It includes radio, TV, film and the growing electronic media—cable, cassettes, videodiscs, holography. It also takes in such diverse "disciplines," as they say in the groves of Academe, as mise-en-scène diffuse lighting to four-walling on a saturation campaign, from A and B cutting to setting up sight gags. The range of terminology can be as relevant to a pratfall as to Prometheus' final speech in the *Prometheus Bound* of Aeschylus.

Why?

Because there is an interrelationship that is conceptually and mimetically basic to all forms of dramaturgy, whatever the hardware of technology or whichever medium is used.

But to the uninitiated this terminology can be disconcerting, even alarming. When anyone who is not part of "the business" is allowed to visit the arcane temple of a motion picture soundstage during the actual ritual of filming a feature motion picture, that visitor may be startled to hear some burly fellow yelling, "Okay! Kill the baby!"

It is important for the visitor to understand that this is not a grisly invitation to infanticide, but simply an informative directive to turn off a small studio lamp. But "lamp" does not mean a table lamp or a standing parlor lamp with an appropriate lampshade. "Lamp" refers to an illuminaire used for lighting the stage. Then too, "stage" does not mean a raised platform for performing in a theater, but is short for "soundstage."

We in the media sometimes forget that we have a special argot, and at parties you can often see director and filming crew talking fervidly of compound moves, swish pans, new film-stocks and ASA ranges; these discussions boring everyone else within hearing range. Media folk can be as enthusiastic and as tedious as yachtsmen, horsey people or wine connoisseurs. Part of this tedium is obviously caused by the exclusionary atmosphere created by the terminology itself. The enthusiasm, however, is endemic to the milieux of media; it has a built-in excitement. This is generated by the emotional agitation of the act of performance, and the awareness that what is being done is for an audience of many thousands to many millions of people. The work will be widespread, and often international in its dissemination.

However, even the communication between and amongst media folk is not always clear. I have personally heard two highly proficient sound mixers, both with considerable years in the business, arguing vehemently over whether or not a final mix should *ever* be called a dubbing session. One said "yes," the other "no." As far as I can determine, after querying many recordists, sound editors and sound company executives, both terms are used for that grand and confusing final sound session, when all the variegated tracks are blended together. Still, "mix" is the preferred term. "Mix" also has its family of variants, "final mix," "mix down," "sound mix," etc.

Context is probably the best guide to using media vocabulary, just as it is in the "real world." Over the years, starting as a child actor, I have worked professionally as actor, writer, director and producer. On many of my documentary shoots, where I was directing and/or producing, I have also worked as an assistant grip. So these terms that I have grown up with in radio, film, TV and the new electronic hardware systems have become part of my daily usage. I have also done time as an English teacher at the college level, and toured as an instructor and seminar speaker in film studies. While doing all this, I have noted variations in the East Coast from West Coast terminology, and Middle American, bewilderment caused by usage that is bordering on obsolescence.

That is why this dictionary has been assembled. It will, hopefully, update the workaday vocabulary of the professionals who work in film, tape, radio or the new media. The definitions have been taught to me directly by working with them first and analyzing them later. I have learned much from the cameramen, grips, producers, soundmen, writers, composers, actors, directors and persons in all the other branches of the arts and crafts that make up this kaleidoscopic business. So this is a dictionary whose vocabulary has been culled from language-at-work.

When Noah Webster brought out his American dictionary in 1806, it was called *A Compendious Dictionary of the English Language*. It had definitions for 37,000 words, including 5000 new ones. As the country grew and changed, so did its language and so did its dictionaries. Today's leading dictionary of American slang has over 22,000 entries.

By the time this dictionary goes from proofreading to editorial correction, and from corrections to the press run, a period of about six months, hundreds of neologisms will make their appearance, many to be evanescent, others to prove more durable. From slang, argot, formal speech, electronic and sociological click-words, to informal speech and colloquialism, new words and compounds will spring up.

With this in mind, to get the most out of this dictionary, we suggest you begin using it right now. These terms are current and prevalent, and for some words, in this hyperaccelerated world of media, obsolescence is just around the corner.

Note: Words in SMALL CAPS indicate cross-references.

A

Aaton: A 16mm camera that can be on a TRIPOD or can be specifically mounted, and is often used HAND-HELD for DOCUMENTARY filming and news-gathering. It has a 400′ MAGAZINE and a variable-speed motor, from 6 to 32 FPS.

ABC: American Broadcasting Company. One of the three major TV networks in the United States. Once an affiliate of NBC.

Aberration: Deviation from the ideal in the performances of LENSES, which impairs the quality of the images they form.

Abrasions: Marks and scratches on the surface of film caused by the contact of the film with an intrusive sharp object. (See also SYNCH MARK)

A.C. (Alternating Current): A current that cyclically reverses its direction. Standard wall-plug current. In opposition to D.C. (direct current). Standard U.S. voltage is 110. For heavier pull—industrial or for driers, ranges, etc.—220 is generally used. These currents vary from country to country.

Academy Awards: The annual awarding of the OSCARS by the ACADEMY OF MOTION PICTURE ARTS AND SCIENCES.

Academy Leader: A type of film LEADER, standardized throughout the industry, which is placed on the beginning and end of all reels or RELEASE PRINTS, and contains THREADING and other information useful to the projectionist. Named after the ACADEMY OF MOTION PICTURE ARTS AND SCIENCES.

Academy of Motion Picture Arts and Sciences: The organization that awards the OSCARS, houses the Margaret Herrick Film Library, sponsors the Student Film Awards, speakers' programs, and in general promotes an upgraded image of the film industry.

Acceptance Angle: Applied to an EXPOSURE METER. The angle of the cone of rays, which the optical design allows to strike the cathode of the photocell.

Account Executive: The person in an advertising agency in charge of a specific "account": "the Ford Motors Account," "the Kellogg account," etc. It is often the account executive who serves as the agency producer on the filming or taping of a commercial.

ACES: The acronym for Automated Camera Effects System, developed by Disney studios, operated by computer to film repeatable camera moves, on separate exposures. Similar cameras at Lucasfilm, Apogee and other SPECIAL EFFECTS houses.

Acetate Base: Standard base for motion picture film composed principally of cellulose acetate. Synonymous with SAFETY BASE.

Acetone: (CH_3COCH_3) Clear, flammable liquid, highly volatile, used to clean filmprint surfaces, SPLICERS and various pieces of editing and camera gear.

Achromatic Lens: A LENS corrected for CHROMATIC ABERRATION by bringing light of two wavelengths to a common focus. All high-quality lenses are achromatic.

Action: A term often used to designate picture in contrast to sound in a REEL of film or tape. Often referred to as the *action track*.

"Action!": The order given by the DIRECTOR of the film when the sound and/or picture cameras are running to speed, cueing the scene to begin.

Action Outline: A written structural form indicating the dramatic physical progression of the film from major SEQUENCE to major sequence, or in a detailed action outline, from SCENE to scene.

Action Viewer: A VIEWFINDER used by a CAMERAMAN, sometimes attached to the camera, which approximates the FRAMING of the LENS. Used to spot action, often in news and DOCUMENTARY situations. It can be used independently by the DIRECTOR to prespot where the camera should be pointed. Used often in sporting events.

Actor: Any person, animal, or, sometimes, product appearing in front of the camera as the subject—or one of the subjects—of the scene or shot. (See also HERO) Any person on-camera in a DOCUMENTARY film, for example, although speaking and appearing as himself or herself is commonly referred to and/or utilized as the "actor." "Actor," in fact, has emerged as the generic term covering all these areas, including the category of ACTRESS. The more restricted term "actor" applies to a person performing a role in any dramatic production in any medium.

Actress: The feminine counterpart of the word "actor." As indicated above, the term actress is sometimes replaced by the basic term ACTOR.

Addressable Converted: TV-set converters that allow the viewer access to special or pay-per-view programs.

Ad-Lib: Jokes, responses, introductory remarks or general commentaries that are improvised; extemporized. However, much "off-the-cuff," and seemingly "spur-of-the-moment," repartee is written and rehearsed material, performed in such a way as to make it look offhand. From the Latin "ad libitum"—at one's pleasure.

ADR (Automated Dialogue Replacement): TV term analogous to film's ELR: DIALOGUE REPLACEMENT. (See also LOOPING)

Advertising-Supported Programming: The great majority of commercial TV programming is paid for by advertisers, in return for which they have their commercials scheduled at preset station-break times or within the viewing time of a particular program. PBS allows "sponsors" or "patrons," i.e., advertisers, to have only an opening and closing credit.

AEA (Actors Equity Association): UNION for actors performing live onstage. Singers and dancers who also act usually have multiple "live" theater affiliations—AEA and AGVA (American Guild of Variety Artists) and/or AGMA (American Guild of Musical Artists).

Aerial Image: Refilming of a film roll of "floating" images, for example, backlit projected images. Often used for film blow-ups or reductions.

AFTRA: See AMERICAN FEDERATION OF TELEVISION AND RADIO ARTISTS.

Agent: Person representing media (see MEDIUM) acting talent, writers, DIRECTORS, CAMERAMEN and other crew members. Staff producers and HYPHENATE PRODUCERS are also often handled by the agent. For services rendered in securing employment interviews, bargaining for fees and contractual advantages, and for general career advice, the agent is paid 10 percent of the talents' gross earnings in their given capacities. Sometimes the agent will also act as business manager, for an additional percentage. This arrangement, however, has tended to decline because of the growing tendency of bifurcation of function between business manager and agent.

Air Time: Segments of time allocated for programming during the broadcasting day. It can be as little as a time purchase for a 10-second commercial to a multihour mini-series, or a regular made-for-TV series. Purchases are made by the ad agencies or time buyers for the client, or sometimes by the production companies directly.

Air-to-Air: Filming or taping of one traveling aircraft from another camera-aircraft that is pacing it. Analogous to PICTURE CAR being filmed/taped by the CAMERA CAR. Air-to-air shots are often made with special aerial mounts. (See also TYLER MOUNT and STEADICAM)

Airwaves: A general term referring to the pathways of all the transmitted broadcasting signals, radio or TV.

Alligator Clamps: Metal spring-clamps with serrated jaws—usually with plastic-covered handles—to hold various objects during the production of a film. For example, to clamp an improvised FLAG or CUTTER to a piece of furniture, while lighting a room; to clamp a blanket between CENTURY STANDS for an on-the-spot sound baffle; to clamp a small tree branch to a century stand to use in front of the camera for a through-the-leaves shot, etc. Alligator clamps developed originally as hot-wiring clamps attached to the end of cables for going straight into electrical power sources.

Amateur: A performer or CREW member who is neither paid nor UNION affiliated. It is also used derogatorily to indicate a person working in media (see MEDIUM) who has a nonprofessional attitude. Another usage is to indicate someone who performs or serves on crew as a hobby or who is new to the professional scene.

Ambience: The general look, feeling or mood infusing the mise-en-scène. In sound, the term refers to exterior or interior PRESENCE: the physical quality of the particular prevailing sound of an area without intrusive DIALOGUE, music or SOUND EFFECTS.

American Broadcasting Company: See ABC.

American Federation of Television and Radio Artists: UNION for performers in radio and TV. The union originally came into prominence in the late 30's as AFRA, American Federation of Radio Artists, and added the "T" for television as TV became a major market for actors right after World War II. SAG and AFTRA have merged forces for medical insurance and credit union loans.

A.M. Light: Early-morning light, with heavily articulated shadows and with skin tones photographing differently than midday or late afternoon. When accompanied by haze not yet burned off by the sun, a special filmic look can be achieved.

Anamorphic Lens: A LENS designed and manufactured to deliberately distort an image to required optical specifications. The lens compresses the image along one axis of the FOCAL PLANE, resulting in a "squeezed" image. By projecting the resultant image through a correcting lens, the ultimate picture emerges as "normal," and usually in a wide-screen format.

Angle Shots: All shots are of course filmed from a specific angle. But, as used in film and TV, an angle shot generally refers to angles other than EYE-LEVEL and HEAD-ON shots. Angles referred to, for example, could be LOW ANGLE, DUTCH ANGLE, extreme CLOSE SHOT, HIGH SHOT, etc.

Animated Graphics System (AGS): A systems technique making it possible to take any VIDEO image and electronically alter it.

Animation: The bringing to apparent movement of inanimate objects set before the camera by employing the joint capacity of film and eye to fuse disparate images into an apparently continuous flow. Among the objects set before the animation camera are cels, cutouts and puppets. *Tabletop animation* is a type of animation in which small objects are photographed in CLOSE-UP and moved along a frame at a time to produce apparent movement.

Animation Camera: The camera used for filming ANIMATION. It is usually mounted on an ANIMATION STAND with its optical axis vertical, so that it looks down on the objects being photographed. The camera-drive meter allows the film to move forward one FRAME at a time.

Animation Stand/Crane: A mechanical device on which to mount a camera in order to move it in precise gradations above an art work peg board or platen. The unit has various built-in capabilities for complex and subtle movements.

Animation Table: Flat table with circular rotary inset to allow cel to be turned to any angle for observation, matching, inking or painting.

Animator: Person who draws, inks or paints animation cels or sheets for animated pictures or who supervises these activities. Today's animators also work with design and production of electronically generated images, through computers and computer tie-ins to other animation devices.

Annie Oakley: A free pass for a motion picture, live performance or a large-screen televised event. The name is derived from the famous markswoman's stunt of throwing a playing card into the air and shooting a hole through it. From this, an "Annie Oakley" came to mean any punched free theatrical ticket or complimentary pass.

Answer Print: First COMPOSITE print from the LAB with sound, music, color (if in color), titles and FADES, DISSOLVES and OPTICAL EFFECTS. In brief, a print potentially ready for release to its target audience. However, there are nearly always visual corrections to be made, and sometimes changes in sound, so that the first answer print is generally a guide to fine-tuning the prints to follow. The answer print therefore usually precedes the first RELEASE PRINT.

A-Page: An inserted additional page in a SCRIPT. Thus, if inserted after page 12, it becomes 12-a. If still another page needs to be added (before page 13), it becomes 12-b, and so on. This allows additions to a script without renumbering.

Aperture, Lens: The opening through which light is admitted to a LENS. The diameter of the aperture in relation to the FOCAL LENGTH and transmission of the lens determines its effective speed.

Aperture Plate: The plate in a camera or projector in close proximity to which the photographic image is exposed or projected. For each gauge of film, the projector aperture is slightly smaller than the camera aperture in order to mask imperfections at the edges of the image and simplify correct FRAMING.

Apochromatic Lens: A LENS corrected for chromatic aberration by bringing light of three wavelengths to a common focus. Lenses designed for accurate copy work are often apochromatic.

Apple Box: Name given to single-unit RISERS, usually made of wood and used to lift people and objects into proper camera range. For example, an actor may be standing on irregular ground and need to be higher than the person he is working with in the scene, or a short actor may need to appear taller than the other actor in the scene. An apple box—probably a half-apple—could be used. An apple box was originally just that, and the size of today's apple box reflects this. The term also came into common usage on the set or location when an actor's height needed to be extended by the half-joking call, "Get an apple box!" or "Put him on an apple box." Today's professional apple boxes are approximately 24″ × 14″ × 8″. A *half-apple* is only 4″ high instead of 8″; a *pancake* only 2″. There is also less-used 6″ height.

Arc Light: In contradistinction to the incandescent lamp, where the light is produced by a heated filament, the illumination from an arc light comes from ionized, glowing gases generated by a burning arc between electrodes. The heat from these arc lights is far more intense than incandescent lamps. The arc lamps work on D.C., but some can work off A.C. as well. The arc-generation of light is used in high-powered lamps for illuminating a set or in some theatrical motion picture projectors. Also called *arc lamp*.

A-Roll/B-Roll Editing: A postproduction term used by editor and LAB in referring to the two ROLLS, arbitrarily marked A and B, which contain alternating segments of the original film and overlap each other when DISSOLVES are needed. The A and B technique allows dissolves and FADES to be made without going through another processing generation. Aside from dissolve-overlap footage, when one roll is running picture, the other is running LEADER and vice versa. Each roll runs the full length of the film. If another roll is added, for the TITLES and/or BURN-INS, the first additional roll is designated "C." If for any reason another roll is needed, it is also designated alphabetically as "D," etc. These are arbitrary letters used for clarity of differentiation. All rolls are separated in the editor's log sheets and given to the lab as instructions for spotting the position and determining the length of dissolves, fades, miscellaneous burn-ins, graphics, titles and CREDITS.

Arri: Common name among filmmakers for an Arriflex camera. Developed originally as a combat camera by the Germans in World War II, it continued on to become an important peacetime news and documentary camera. Its use became more widespread as the camera developed faster blimping (see BLIMP) capacity and, eventually, self-blimped status. The 16mm versions are used for industrials, commercials, DOCUMENTARIES and news-gathering; the 35mm models are used for commercials and feature films, and sometimes documentary and industrial films. Conversely, the 16mm blimped models are occasionally used for feature films shot in 16mm or SUPER-16 and blown up into 35mm.

Art Director: Person in charge of the physical "look" of the film. His or her duties comprise any or all of the following, depending upon the nature of the project: making preliminary sketches, drawing STORY BOARDS, color-coordinating scenic PROPS with one another and/or with wardrobe, sketching basic scenic designs, consulting with lighting GAFFER and director of photography on illumination CHROMA, working with or acting as graphics designer to give film a cohesive visual style; also, in some cases, actually selecting and making purchases of the scenic props.

ASA Index: A measurement of a specific FILM STOCK's sensitivity to light. ASA originally stood for American Standard Association, which is now the American National Standards Institute, Inc. Rarely, however, will a filmmaker speak of the "ANSI range," the common working terms being "ASA range," "ASA number," "ASA rating," "ASA speed," etc., all of which are interchangeable. The greater the sensitivity to light, the greater the ASA number: an ASA rating of 100 will have twice the light sensitivity of a film with a 50 ASA rating.

Aspect Ratio: The ratio of width-to-height of a motion picture FRAME. The original 35mm ratio before wide-screen was 1 × 1:33, a ratio reflected approximately in TV screen images (16mm, other than SUPER-16mm, uses the 1 × 1:33 aspect ratio).

Assembly: Editing the WORKPRINT shots of a film into approximately the right order. (See also ROUGH CUT and FINE CUT)

Assistant Director: In a small production unit, his or her chief function is to act as liaison with authorities and with suppliers of services. In a large unit, he or she is responsible for the presence of actors at the right time and place and for carrying out the DIRECTOR's instructions.

Associate Producer: A production assistant who helps with BUDGETS, scouting, casting and all other production duties, working directly with the PRODUCER.

Asynchronous Sound: Sound related directly to the action, not synchronized to the exact FRAME, but laid in as BACKGROUND sound or off-screen sound.

A-Team: Working name for the on-camera actors or STUNTPERSONS who will perform the actual scene, regarded as a separate unit from the STAND-INS who help the camera crew set up the shot. Also called *first string*.

Atmosphere: EXTRAS, as a group. Comparable to supers in live theater.

Audio: A designation for sound in general, as in *audio engineering*. In two-column SCRIPTS the left-hand column is usually designated "audio" and the right column "VIDEO," or sometimes "picture" or "visual."

Audiovisual: A term to designate a total approach to sight-and-sound presentation of information. Used less frequently in referring to entertainment films and tapes. Many schools and large businesses utilize AV centers, the former to augment basic visual education, the latter for IN-HOUSE training or general motivation.

Audition: A reading or tryout in which performers read DIALOGUE from sides or scripts, sing, dance or display the particular talent for which they are being considered by the DIRECTOR and/or PRODUCER.

Auteur Theory: The faddish theory, now obsolescent, that the DI-RECTOR is the true "author" of the film, whether he or she wrote it or not. Based on a concept, and often a misunderstanding, in interviews with French and Italian NEW WAVE directors.

Automatic Exposure: An exposure-setting device self-activated by intensity of light entering the LENS.

B

Baby: A lighting unit next in size below a JUNIOR, using a 1000-watt bulb. A *baby door* is the BARN DOOR for this lamp.

Background: A word indicating people, objects, set pieces and scenery that form the setting against which the foreground players and action are set. An EXTRA is also referred to as a *background player*. In sound, background means the general aural ambience of the scene plus specific distant sounds present during filming or added in postproduction: a dog barking a few blocks away, a far-off siren, a foghorn in the bay, etc.

Backlighting: Illumination coming from sources behind performers or objects in relation to the camera eye. (See also LIGHTING, 1.)

Barn Door: Hinged door mounted on a studio LAMP, which may be swung to block off light from an area where it is not wanted or to pinpoint a source of light.

Barney: A heavy-matted cloth covering for a sound camera, designed to deaden the drive-mechanism sound of the camera when it is running. Evidently the name derives from the comic strip character Barney Google. But whether it stemmed from the two humps and drive wheels on the camera MAGAZINE to be covered, which resembled Barney Google's big eyes, or from the lumpy look of his horse with horse blanket on, is conjectural.

Bar Sheets: A chart used in ANIMATION that indicates the number of FRAMES for each recorded syllable of DIALOGUE, as well as the pauses. Also called *lead sheets*.

Base Film: The transparent material on which a photographic emulsion is coated is called film base. It serves no photographic purpose, but acts as a support for the thin emulsion layer. For this reason, it is sometimes called the *support*. Safety base is now in universal use; before 1947, nitrate (flammable) base was standard for 35mm film.

Batch: The quantity of emulsion manufactured at any one time for the production of RAW STOCK is substantially the same, and the stock on which it is coated is called a batch. Different batches of film, however, may differ appreciably in their characteristics. For this reason, sensitometric tests are always made on a piece of film from the same batch as the film to be processed, since batch variations often necessitate the use of correction filters.

Batten: Horizontal lengths of wood or pipe, rigged above the SET on ropes/cables and pulley. Used for flying scenery or for mounting overhead lights. Originated in live theater.

Beam Projector: A LIGHTING device that projects a single pattern of light, such as an infrared beam, a laser beam or a focused-light beam with variable color frames, for example, a FOLLOW SPOT. This is to be differentiated from MOTION PICTURE PROJECTOR.

Bell and Howell: Motion picture equipment manufacturer of cameras, projectors and accessories. A pioneer and leader—with Eastman Kodak—in the development of the 8mm and the 16mm markets. The 8mm format—now Super-8—is used primarily for home movies, while 16mm is used for news-gathering and DOCUMENTARY filming. Also, some low-budget feature films are made in 16mm and blown up to 35mm, to be released as 35mm theatrical prints. (See also SUPER-16)

Best Boy: GRIP and electrical term. Second-in-command on the electrical or grip crews.

BG: The abbreviation for BACKGROUND.

Billing: The sequence, position and size of a performer or crew member's CREDITS on the screen and in advertisements. For example, how large is a name to appear on the screen? Will it be alone on a single card or a shared credit? Will it be on a credit roll at the end of the film? Will it or will it not be included on posters, ads or releases?

Bin: A container for film, often with sorting peg rack, for film segments. Usually made of fire-resistant material. Placed in CUTTING ROOMS and other rooms where film is handled. Usually on wheels. Scrap film is dumped into a *wastebin*.

Binaural Reproduction: A reproduction transmission sound system in which the conditions of binaural (normal human reception) hearing are reproduced as closely as possible. Sometimes this term is applied to a two-channel system, the term *stereophonic reproduction* being reserved for systems employing three or more channels.

Binocular Vision: The possession by human beings of two eyes separated by a distance of about two and a half inches (interocular distance) and having overlapping fields. Of great assistance in sizing the distance of objects as near or far from the observer. *Image system:* A pictorial system based on binocular vision is called *stereoscopic* (3-D); one not so based, *planoscopic* (flat).

Bipack: To superimpose TITLES or other images over another piece of BACKGROUND film.

Bipack Printing: A film-print process wherein two pieces of film are run through together in contact, for matting or DOUBLE EXPOSURE.

Bit: 1. A small part in a film or tape show. The person doing the part is called a *bit player*. 2. A preset visual or verbal gag within a comedy routine. 3. A discrete unit of data in computer technology.

Black and White Reproduction: A form of photographic process in which color is translated into a scale of monochromatic densities ranging from near opacity to near transparency. When the photographic image is viewed on a white screen, it appears in the scale of near-black and near-white, the range of tonalities determining the contrast of the image.

Blackout: 1. Sudden switching off of scenic lights instead of dimming them down. Used as a "light curtain," particularly at the end of COM-

EDY sketches in a revue or variety format. 2. A COMEDY sketch written with a curtain line strong enough to justify a light blackout.

Blimp: The soundproof housing that surrounds a camera used to record DIALOGUE, and which prevents the camera noise from being picked up by the microphone on sound takes. *Self-blimped* cameras are those in which the normal housing silences the noise of the drive mechanism, without the addition of an external blimp.

Block Booking: In distribution, the placement of a group of film prints in various theaters in a specific, concentrated area.

Blocking: The coordination and setting of movements by actors in a scene. Blocking—in film and video—utilizes floor marks and other spotting devices to make sure the actor hits the same spot on the same dialogue. (See also MARKS)

Bloop: The punchout, the PATCH, FOGGING mark, painted area or stencil by which the "bloop" (noise made by the SPLICE in joining two pieces of SOUND TRACK) is rendered inaudible. The process of applying the bloop is therefore known either as BLOOPING or *de-blooping*, the meaning of the two terms being identical.

Blooping: Any method of silencing unwanted noise produced by the passage of a SPLICE through a sound reproducer. (See also BLOOP)

Blooping Patch: A small opaque piece of material fixed over a sound SPLICE in order to BLOOP it.

Blow-up: The optical printing process by which a picture image on a smaller gauge of film is produced from one on a larger gauge of film. A common application is the production of 35mm separation negatives from 16mm monopack color originals. Blow-up also refers to the enlargement of the film image in an optical camera.

BO (Box Office): 1. The cubicle in which the ticket sellers work. 2. General term for money from admissions. 3. An attractive draw at the box office: "He's just not box office."

The Boards: As in "treading the boards": working onstage in live theater. The physical STAGE itself.

Body Brace: A specially designed camera mount for HAND-HELD shots using various frame-mount designs and configurations. It is supported against the body for greater camera stability. (See also STEADICAM)

Bonus Print: A term used by educational/informational film distributors to describe an extra film print or VIDEOTAPE given as a bonus for a large purchase of prints.

Booking: Contracting and fixing performance runs for live talent, films or any theatrical/entertainment event. The person who sets deals for obtaining live talent for a club, a show or an event is known as a *booking agent*.

Boom, Camera: A mobile camera mount, usually of a large size, on which the camera may be made to extend out over the set/or raised above it. Provision is made for counterbalancing, raising and lowering, rotating, and bodily moving the boom, these motions being effected either by electrical motors or by hand.

Boom, Microphone: A simple version of the camera boom (see BOOM, CAMERA), designed to project the microphone over the set and twist it in any direction required by the MIXER.

Booster Light: Artificial light used to augment daylight in an exterior scene.

Box Office: See BO.

Breakaway Props: Includes breakaway chairs made of balsa wood or mallow-pith derivatives, and breakaway glass windows and bottles made of safe-shattering plastic. Used to create effects of shattering without the attendant dangers.

Break(ing) Down: In cutting, the act of reducing a ROLL of film into its component shots. This term is usually applied to rushes when a single roll of picture or sound may contain thirty or more separate scenes and takes.

Breathing: A pulsating in-and-out of a projected film image, causing an unsteady focus of the picture. There are any number of causes, such as film buckling in camera while shooting, film buckling in the projector, or an unstable APERTURE gate in the projector.

Bridge: A music cue used to carry us from one scene or one mood to another.

B-Roll: See A-ROLL/B-ROLL EDITING.

Brute: A large ARC LIGHT that works on direct current only.

Budget: 1. The *adjusted budget* is the revised budget based on new items and cost increases in existing ones. Also includes finalization of open items. 2. The *estimate budget* is a rough budget, approximating production cost, based on industry fees and percentages, and projecting preproduction, production and postproduction schedules. 3. The *prelim budget* is a more detailed budget than the estimate budget, probably with more of the above-the-line items established and indicated, and all of the below-the-line costs quoted and tallied. 4. The *production budget* is a fully detailed one, running about twenty-four pages, itemized as closely as possible and used as a guide to help control production expenses. Used by PRODUCERS, unit and production managers, as well as department heads and the DIRECTOR.

Burn-in: A superimposition of white TITLES, lettering or graphic images. If color is to be added, the burn-in must be black-matted and filmed separately. A common burn-in is in DOCUMENTARIES, when the name of the on-camera person who is speaking appears, usually in the lower center portion of the screen.

Business: Additional directed action in a film or tape that augments and strengthens the existing theme or idea of a dramatic work.

Busy: Too much BUSINESS. Distracting and random movement within a scene; over-full of people and things.

Butt Splice: An editor's film SPLICE wherein film ends are joined together without overlapping.

Buy: 1. A good TAKE. An acceptance, for example, at the completion of a SCENE, "That's a buy!" To indicate "That's a buy" can also mean that an entire production concept is agreed upon and can proceed into the production-contract phase. 2. "A buy" can also mean "That's it; it's a wrap": the production is completed. (See also WRAP)

B-Winds: See WINDS.

C

Cable: General term for TV system wherein picture and sound are transmitted directly over phone lines and then switched from a local junction near the individual homes to separate cables leading into each household. Cable systems are extra to install, and usually charge a monthly fee for the use of their specific multichannel service. Cable systems are also used within large governmental or corporate buildings for in-house telecasting and in hotels and motels for closed-circuit programming.

Cable-Access Channels: Franchised channels with 3500 or more subscribers specifically designated for use in public-access programming. All requests must be handled in a nondiscriminatory manner, no prejudice to be shown because of race, sex, national origin, political affiliation or religion. Also, requests are to be processed in order received. Programming is for the community audience of the particular geographical viewing area.

Cable Household: Marketing and general audience–survey term, designating a home that has some form of cable TV.

Cable Penetration: A ratio count of homes with TV in proportion to those with cable TV. The number of homes in the given area tied in to a cable-TV system.

Cable-Ready TV: A basic TV monitor with integrated coaxial input jacks to accommodate the HVF tuner. Such tie-in jacks make it easy to add on cable-system units to the TV set.

Cable TV: See CABLE.

Calibration: The markings on LENS barrels and rings, used to set the effective APERTURE of the lens diaphragm and to control the FOCUS.

Camera: Any lightproof box for exposing film.

Camera Angle: The field of view of a camera when it is set up to shoot. The qualifying terms *high, low,* and *wide* are based on an imaginary norm that roughly corresponds to a 35mm camera with a 2-inch lens pointed at a scene from shoulder height.

Camera Car: Any car, truck or customized vehicle designed to handle special camera mounts and/or customized BOOMS. Used for TRAVELING SHOTS and FOLLOW SHOTS and/or to be able to move rapidly from place to place while on LOCATION. Most professional cameras have a preset camera boom seated on the working platform of the camera "car," this so-called car often being basically a flatbed truck holding or carrying the boom. Also called an *insert car.* (See also PICTURE CAR)

Cameraman: General term for any member of the camera crew, particularly the *director of photography* and the *camera operator.* 1. The *first cameraman*, often called the *director of photography* or *chief cameraman*, is responsible for the movements and setting of the camera and for the LIGHTING of the scene being shot. Except in small units, he or she does not as a rule manipulate the camera controls, either when making preliminary adjustments or during actual shooting. 2. The *second cameraman*, often called the *assistant cameraman* or *camera operator*, acts under instructions from the first cameraman, carries out the preliminary adjustments to the camera, and monitors the scene during shooting. 3. The first assistant cameraman is chief assistant to the camera operator. Often responsible for following FOCUS. 4. The *second assistant cameraman* is the second assistant to the camera operator. 5. The *still cameraman* is responsible for the taking of publicity and production still photographs.

Camera, Motion Picture: Types: 1. A *combat camera* is one designed primarily for HAND-HELD shooting under combat conditions. 2. A *field camera* is a nonsilenced camera primarily adapted to shooting exterior scenes, where portability is of first importance. 3. A *studio* *camera* is one designed for studio use, fully silenced and carrying every refinement needed for SYNCH-SOUND filming.

Camera Mount: Any camera-holding device that allows panning (see PAN) or TILTING. The mounts are attached to TRIPODS, flatboards, DOLLIES, BOOMS or customized mount-holders. A body brace or a STEADICAM are camera mounts.

Camera Movement: 1. Movement of the whole camera as a unit (nonpivotal movement on its horizontal or vertical axes) while shooting a scene. 2. See also INTERMITTENT MOVEMENT.

Camera Original: Film exposed in the camera.

Camera Right/Camera Left (Screen Right/Screen Left): East-west orientation for use by writers, directors, cameramen and editors to help them establish patterns of filmically consistent movement. Analogous to *stage left* and *stage right* in live theater. However, stage right is to the right of the performer as he or she looks out into the audience and stage left is to his or her left in that same position. *Camera right/left* or *screen right/left* are just the reverse, that is, from the point of view of the audience. Anything right of center, as the camera or audience sees it, is considered camera or screen right, or, if to the left, camera or screen left. These directions have cultural and symbolic meanings not to be found on the live stage. For example, a train moving from right to left is always assumed to be moving west; left to right, east.

Camera Riser: Any platform or shoring-up support that takes the camera higher than eye-level, from floor or ground base.

Camera Tracks: Tracks of wood or metal laid down to carry a DOLLY or camera BOOM in order to ensure smoothness of camera movement.

Camera Wedge: Flat sliver of wood with triangular ends used to secure improvised rigging of a camera or to lock off a camera position. Carried by the assistant cameraman (see under CAMERAMAN, 2) or head GRIP.

Candlepower: Measurement unit used in evaluating light intensity. In media (see MEDIUM), used especially by directors of photography or lighting GAFFER when lighting a set. What is measured is the strength of white light in the specific area to be filmed/taped. Originally "candlepower" came from the fact that the light-strength unit was derived from a spermaceti candle burning at the rate of 120 grams per hour. (See also LIGHTING)

Carousel (Carrousel): Multiple 35mm slide holder in a circular (carousel) form that holds and projects slides in any desired sequence. The basic tool of the MIXED MEDIA shows, used in conjunction with elements such as live performers, film projectors, light-beam projectors, audio units, etc.

Car Pass: See DRIVE-ON PASS.

Cast: Noun: The total number of performers that comprise the requisite demand to fill all roles indicated in a particular film, tape, radio program, or whatever dramatic medium is selected. In film this generally breaks down into these categories: STARS, FEATURE PLAYERS, BIT and/or DAY PLAYERS. The BACKGROUND cast—comparable to supernumeraries on stage (supers)—would be the EXTRAS, also referred to as ATMOSPHERE. Special cast categories would be actors in cameos and STUNTPEOPLE. (See also STAND-IN) In musicals there would be further subcategories of dancer and singer. Verb: To select actors for various roles in a program. Often handled by the CASTING DIRECTOR.

Casting Department: A regular division of major film or TV studios, as well as larger independent production companies, specializing in casting the dramatic or musical projects of these companies.

Casting Director: Person in charge of sending out requests for actors to come read for roles in SCRIPTS to be produced or already in production. The CASTING DIRECTOR works closely with the DIRECTOR and sometimes the PRODUCER in setting up the readings. Final selection of performers is by the director, or by producer. In casting for COMMERCIALS or INDUSTRIAL FILMS, the client often makes the ultimate choice.

Cathode Ray Tube (CRT): The basic TV-tube that evolved from the simpler diode, but in more complex form. It includes an electron gun that emits a stream of electrons which strike a coated-fluorescent tube widened at the other end: the TV "screen." When activated, the electron gun emits its grid-controlled electron stream, which forms— or "reassembles"—the picture.

CBS: Major radio network that became along with ABC and NBC one of the big three of TV.

Cello: A type of glass having an indented cellular pattern which enables it to act as a diffuser. The term cello is often applied to the diffuser made of this substance. Used in LIGHTING.

Celluloid: The working name for cellulose nitrate, which was the original flammable film base, now replaced by ACETATE-BASE film.

Cement, Film: A liquid used for dissolving film base in order to make two pieces of film unite in a SPLICE.

Censorship: Arbitrary applied guidelines as to what can or cannot be said or shown in the performing media arts, the criteria differing widely from medium to medium and within the medium itself.

Central Casting: First casting service to provide the studios with specific types of EXTRAS: American Indians, wrestlers, swimmers, executives at conference table, etc. These services were paid for by the production company or the studio production unit. The fee paid is based on the percentage of the extra's gross pay. Since Central Casting there have been many other casting companies and services established.

Century Stand: Basic metal all-purpose stand, with a special head on top, to which can be attached arms for flags, CUCALORISES, tree branches, or whatever is called for. Also small lights: an INKY-DINK light is often cantilevered from a c-stand arm to move into, above or below the scene. Small lights can also be attached by slipping over the topmost vertical rod extension of the century stand. Also called *c-stand*.

Change Focus: See FOLLOW FOCUS and RACK FOCUS.

Changeover: The immediate switch of sound-and-picture on one REEL to that of the following reel, mounted on another projector during a film showing.

Changeover Cue: This is a circular mark in the upper right-hand corner of a few FRAMES just before the end of a reel of film. There are two warnings, which sometimes activate an audio signal inside the projection room, to give the projectionist time to line up FOCUS and activate the projector-to-projector changeover.

Changing Bag: A lightproof bag usually with two light-trap sleeves where the CAMERAMAN's arms (generally the assistant cameraman) can slip into the bag with the roll of film and magazine and change film in this portable surrogate darkroom. The bags are made of cloth (sometimes plastic) reinforced with lightproof materials and often waterproof. It is not uncommon in using the smaller cameras where the magazine is self-contained—Bolexes, Beaulieus, etc.—to put the entire camera into the bag for the film change.

Character Actor/Actress: Performer who portrays supporting roles. This differs from the more romantic leads—INGENUE, JUVENILE, leading lady, or leading man. The character actors are often older than the leads, or of different nationalities. Sometimes, as in the Western hero's sidekick, the character actor serves as comedy relief. Great character performers of the past would certainly include Marie Dressler, Wallace Beery, George Arliss, Mischa Auer, Herman Bing, and Margaret Dumont. It is the function of the character actor to give added texture to a given drama or comedy.

Characterization: The internal and external delineation by an actor of the character he or she is portraying. Characterization derives from three areas: the SCRIPT itself, with the human background environment and personality of each character; the additional interpretative touches added by the DIRECTOR; the final subjective fusing of these elements by the actor; and the physicalization of this fusion in performance.

Checkerboard Cutting: An editing technique that does away with the unwanted image of the frame-cut line. This is done by covering the immediate FRAMES on either side of the frame line with black LEADER. By doing this, the transfer of the "splice-image"—emulsion, tape, or frame line—is eliminated. Called checkerboard because of the alternating frames of picture and black leader.

Chicken Coop: A rectangular lighting instrument with multiple globes, covered with wire mesh; usually the same sort of mesh used in chicken coops.

Chroma: Color-saturation term, indicating the amount of saturation of any particular color.

Chroma Key: A TV-production matting technique, done electronically.

Chromatic Aberration: A LENS aberration characterized by the failure of a lens to bring light of different wavelengths to the same FOCUS.

Cinch Marks: Lateral scratch marks on the surface of a piece of film, usually made by pressing down on the edges of a lightly wound roll of film or drawing the roll tight.

Cinemascope: Wide-screen system developed by MGM, utilizing ANAMORPHIC filming and projecting units.

Cinéma Verité: A realistic approach, basically without directorial intervention, of an event. The event could be anything from a confrontation of man-to-wife in argument to a mass rally of thousands of people. *Woodstock*, in part, was cinéma verité. The on-camera interviews would be more straight DOCUMENTARY style. Many documentaries are in part cinéma verité, but the term is used generally to refer to films that are totally in this style or to fictional films that simulate undirected reality.

Cinerama: Initially a three-camera, three-projector and matching three-screen system for maximum images, augmented by stereophonic sound.

Clapper Boards: A pair of hinged boards that are clapped together in DIALOGUE shooting before or after each TAKE, when the picture camera and sound camera are running at synchronous speed. The first FRAME of closure on the picture is afterward synchronized in the CUTTING ROOM with the modulations resulting from the sound of the hinged boards clapping together, thus establishing synchronism between SOUND TRACK and picture tracks. (See also SLATE BOARD)

Clapper boards have been dispensed with in some modern, large-scale types of sound-recording systems.

Claw: A device used in cameras for providing motion. The claw engages one or more SPROCKET holes, and thus pulls down the film a distance equal to the height of the frame; it then withdraws to go back to the initial position. This claw pull-down mechanism is also a standard feature of many projectors.

Clean Entrance/Exit: An actor or object coming into FRAME from being totally outside its field of vision, or vice versa, that is, exiting the frame completely.

Clear: Return to head of tape and to zero-count. To erase the tape by DEGAUSSING or recording over it directly.

Clearance: Permission to utilize registered and/or copyrighted material in film or TV. Materials such as music, film clips, long quotations, etc.

Click Track: A film LOOP of a specific length, set to metronome equivalents, marked by an audible click. Used in musically scoring a motion picture. If there is to be irregular or broken rhythm within a sequence, for example, a dance number, the editor will scratch the synchronous WORKPRINT used for SCORING on the track itself. When scoring the film, the conductor listens to the click through headphones so that the click sounds will not be recorded with the music.

Cliff-hanger: A film of suspense through action, usually building to a high climax. So named from the old silent serials, comedies and dramas where, just before the end of the film, the actor or actress in distress was rescued, often hanging from a cliff.

Climax: That part of a dramatic work in which the action reaches its most intense and decisive moment.

Clip: A short piece of film cued in to live TV programming.

Clock: To time a scene, segment or entire show.

Close: Noun: The windup of a variety act or show. Verb: "Let's close with a big ending."

Closed Circuit: A private TV line or lines for professional viewing or for placement in theaters for events not on regular TV. These commercial aspects of direct-line monitoring are now rapidly being replaced by individual home-use via CABLE and satellite.

Closed Set: A TV or motion picture soundstage or exterior SET that is open to immediate cast and crew and closed to visitors and to those not directly involved with the production.

Close Shot: A SHOT where we are in close to the action. Not usually as tight as a CLOSE-UP. Between a MEDIUM SHOT and a CLOSE-UP.

Close-up: Head-and-shoulders shot of a performer. A *tight close-up* is the head only. An extreme *close-up* (abbreviated ECU or XCU) could be eyes or lips only.

Coated Lens: A camera LENS, the exterior side of which is chemically coated to reduce reflection. This magnesium fluoride application allows more light to pass through the lens and onto the emulsion surface of the film.

Cobweb-Maker/Spinner: A SPECIAL EFFECTS device, with fan connected to a container for the rubber cement. Works electrically to blow strands of rubber cement onto a specified set area, to give the appearance of cobwebs.

Code Numbers: Identical numbers printed during the editorial process along the edges of synchronized positive picture and SOUND TRACKS, thus in effect providing SYNC MARKS at intervals of one foot from the start of the reel. To be carefully distinguished from NEGATIVE NUMBERS.

Coding Machine: A machine that prints matching numbers on the picture track and the SOUND TRACK in order to facilitate synching (see SYNCHRONISM).

Cold Lights: Fluorescent lamps.

Color: 1. The nuances and shading of an actor in line readings, gestures and movement; the added personal emphasis given to a role by the performer. 2. In writing, color is the variegated range of the text in interrelationship to its depth-of-a-concept, the basis of which is the responsibility of directors and performers to delineate.

Color Bars: VIDEO varicolored stripes to check and correct color before broadcasting or presenting a tape for viewers on any viewing system. Precedes the actual program section of a tape and runs for 10 seconds to a minute.

Colorblind Film: A type of film with black and white emulsion that responds to one only region of the spectrum, usually the blue, and is therefore unable to distinguish colors on a monochromatic scale.

Color Temperature: A value scale for measuring a light source in degrees Kelvin. A degree Kelvin uses the centigrade scale, but its 0° starts at − 273° centigrade.

Color Wheel: A rotating wheel of various circular frames for holding color GELS that can rotate at a steady rate for continued color changes or be used to switch rapidly from one color to another. For special on-camera or onstage LIGHTING effects.

Columbia Pictures: For many years located in Hollywood's "Gower Gulch" as a maker of quickies. Frank Capra's and later Orson Welles' films were greatly instrumental in raising it to the level of a major motion picture studio. It shares production facilities at Warner Brothers Studios, now called The Burbank Studios.

Comeback: To return to a successful career in film or TV after having been absent for a considerable time.

Comedy: Subject approach using caricature, slapstick, satire, farce, plot situations, bawdiness, grotesquery, parody or wit. All of these to be used for a total humorous result.

Coming Attractions: Also called *trailers*. Short excerpted and assembled segments of a film or tape, edited for maximum impact with added graphics and/or special scenes. It is essentially a commercial for an upcoming or current movie or TV program.

Commercial: Adjective: A descriptive word indicating sales power of a film program, a series or a general media concept: "It's a good story but it's not commercial." Noun: A radio or TV ad broadcast during COMMERCIAL BREAKS.

Commercial Break: A time slot allocated during or between programs for a commercial and/or public service announcement.

Compilation Film: Film comprised mostly or completely of preshot footage, such as news coverage, OUTS, pickup shots or technical shots. The editing of it is after-the-fact, sometimes to a script or detailed outline.

Completion Services: Also known as *Postproduction services*. These include LOOPING, sound transfers, lab printing, conforming of original picture, graphics, mixing (see MIX), etc.

Composite: The presence on one piece of film of corresponding sound and picture images, either in editorial, camera or projection SYNCHRONISM.

Composite Dupe Negative: A COMPOSITE NEGATIVE which, after exposure and processing, produces a dupe negative picture and SOUND TRACK image.

Composite Master Positive: A COMPOSITE print usually made for the purpose of producing composite or picture and sound dupe negatives to be used for printing RELEASE PRINTS.

Composite Negative: A NEGATIVE film that is exposed and processed to produce both SOUND TRACK and picture negative images on the same film.

Composite Print: A positive film having both picture and SOUND TRACK images on the same film.

Compound Move: Movement of both camera and actors within a scene. Also refers to a multiple move, for example, the camera may be TILTING, PANNING, and zooming (see ZOOM) all at the same time.

Comps: Short for *complimentary tickets and/or passes*. Nearly all press coverage of a film is on comps. Tickets to watch a TV show being taped are comps.

Computer Graphics: Optical images and SPECIAL EFFECTS created by electronically programmed units and used in film, TV, videocassette software, HOLOGRAPHY or mixed media.

Conflict: The confrontation between protagonist and the antagonist or antagonistic forces: Man-Against-Man, Man-Against-the-World, Man-Against-Forces of Evil, Man-Against-Nature, etc. Elements of opposition and struggle within the plot framework.

Console: A control panel, used for sound recording and re-recording, which enables the input from one or more microphones or DUBBERS to be varied in amplitude and frequency. It also makes provision for the MIXER to monitor the signal at the console output. Re-recording consoles are often of impressive appearance and carry fifty or more controls.

Continuity: The dramatically structured sequence of events in a film or tape production.

Continuity Cutting: A style of cutting marked by its emphasis on maintaining the continuous and seemingly uninterrupted flow of action in a story, as if this action were being observed by the audience as spectator. Contrasted with DYNAMIC CUTTING. (See also FILM CONTINUITY)

Continuity Editing: Editing a film that is shot in continuity (see CONTINUITY SHOOTING) or editing in script sequence and leadering the areas where scenes are still to be added.

Continuity Shooting: Shooting the SCRIPT in the scene sequence in which it is written. Entire films are seldom shot this way, but the long, going-downriver sequence in the film classic *Deliverance* was actually done in this manner. TV soaps (see SOAP OPERA) are taped in continuity, often as an uninterrupted live performance.

Contract Player: A player under contract to a studio or production company who works on programs or films as assigned.

Contrapuntal Sound: Sound or music that increases dramatic or comedic intensity by "playing against the scene." It often conflicts directly with the mood of the action. For example, a light, happy tune that a young boy whistled in earlier scenes might be played over a scene of his funeral, the lilting little melody playing in counterpoint to the tragic surroundings being far more potent than "tragic" music.

Contrast: In a scene, this term popularly denotes the difference between the brightness of the most illuminated and the least illuminated areas; and, in a NEGATIVE or print, the difference between the densities of the most exposed (see EXPOSURE) and least exposed areas. Generally measured in gamma.

Cordless Sync, Crystal Sync, Cableless Sync: Terms for sound-recording units that can maintain synchronous (see SYNCHRONISM) camera-to-recorder sound without being physically connected by a synch-pulse cable.

Core: Centers, usually made of plastic, upon which RAW STOCK is wound. Developed NEGATIVE is usually stored on cores rather than REELS. Cores are divided by film size and are "male" or "female" depending upon the center-hole stamping.

Costume Designer: Person who sketches the general "look" of costumes to be worn by the actors in a film or TV productions. Good costumes not only enhance the richness of the particular role, but can also comment on the personality of the character portrayed.

Costumer: One responsible for obtaining, classifying and fitting costumes in preproduction and during filming/taping.

Counter: A numerical meter that counts film length in feet, tape in numbers of FRAMES, etc., and registers these numbers on a dial or readout unit.

Courtesy Pass: Sometimes a COMP ticket, sometimes a specially issued pass or a reduced-price ticket.

Cover: Noun: A camera hood or wrapping to keep out dust, moisture and inclemencies of weather. Verb: 1. To visually film/tape an event with its concomitant sound. 2. To place the camera in such a way that it can pick up the necessary action.

Coverage: 1. In dramatic film or tape, additional shots to augment the MASTER SHOT, such as SINGLES, CUTAWAY SHOTS and tight TWO-SHOTS. It is from the master shot and coverage that the editor builds his or her scenes. 2. In DOCUMENTARIES and news, the term "coverage" means total tape or film used to record a particular event.

Crab Dolly: Wheeled camera-mount that can be steered. Generally, it has a vertical metal adjustable column for raising or lowering the camera.

Cradle: A device to support heavy lenses. It gives the LENS greater stability and protects it from damage. It also protects the lens mount from being bent or ruptured from the weight of the lens.

Crane: A large, vehicular BOOM that allows the camera to move in a wide, circular movement or move up for a HIGH SHOT in a vertical, diagonal or irregular path. Allows for great flexibility of camera movement.

Crawl Titles: TITLES or CREDITS that appear to "roll in" from the bottom of the frame and exit at the top. It is also the name for the mechanical device on which the credits/titles are mounted and filmed/taped. Also called *roll-up titles* or *creeper titles*.

Credits: The listed names of the CAST, CREW and STAFF involved in a given film or TV production that are seen at the beginning and/or end. Live theater credits are given in printed programs, and radio credits are spoken by the announcer.

Credit Sheet: A typed, photocopied or printed sheet or sheets giving the background of a performer, DIRECTOR, PRODUCER or CREW/staff member. It lists the past productions on which the person has worked, what his or her role or function was, and also indicates the most recent CREDITS. Also called *bio sheet*.

Crew: The crew is composed of those who work "behind the camera": soundmen, CAMERAMAN, GRIPS, etc. Differentiated from the CAST.

Crew Call: Typed or photocopied notice either hand-delivered by the ASSISTANT DIRECTOR or PRODUCTION MANAGER, and/or posted on the CREW's production board. It gives the names of those called and where and when the filming/taping is to be.

Critical Focus: Precision-sharp clarity of image. Also an indication that such clarity is mandatory in a specified shot.

Crop: To cut off visual information by FRAMING, either accidentally or deliberately. Still photographers often crop their NEGATIVES in order to intensify the image. Also a direction: "Crop off more of the top of the house in the framing so I can see all the steps."

Cross-Fade: (Radio/Film) Basically an AUDIO term to indicate the lowering of the sound of an outgoing scene—usually to the level of inaudibility—while increasing the volume of the incoming scene.

Crutch Tips: One-inch rubber caps to cover the ends of crutches. Used by GRIPS to place on CENTURY STAND legs, especially in on-location shooting, to keep the metal legs from scratching hardwood, plastic or marble, or from snagging carpeting.

Crystal Motor: Electric unit with speed regulated by a vibrating crystal. Used to maintain CORDLESS SYNC or CRYSTAL SYNC.

Crystal Sync: SYNC SOUND system allowing DOUBLE-SYSTEM SOUND RECORDING without cables and still maintaining synchronous speed with the camera. This is done with a precise and constant frequency-reference signal.

CS: The abbreviation for CLOSE SHOT.

CU: The abbreviation for CLOSE-UP.

Cucaloris (Cookie): Pronounced ku-kah-lor-iss. Also spelled and referred to as *kookaloris, kuke* and *cookeloris*. A shading device with a cut-out vermicular pattern used in LIGHTING to create a mottled light effect by placing it in front of the proper source. Often simulates blurred leafy shadows.

Cue: A signal by word or action to an actor for his/her next speech, reaction or movement.

Cue Mark: A scratch mark, editor's crayon mark or punched hole on a piece of film or magnetic sound track, serving as a start mark for LOOPING, editing or in an INTERLOCK SYSTEM.

Cut: An instantaneous transition from any shot to the immediately succeeding shot, from splicing (see SPLICE) the two shots together.

"Cut!": The order given by the DIRECTOR of the film when the action in a shot is completed, to indicate that the sound and/or pictures are to be shut off. Or to stop "wild" sound recording. (See also "WILD" RECORDING)

Cut: (Delete) To omit or remove DIALOGUE from a SCRIPT, a piece of action when on the SET, or a segment of film when editing. Used both as noun and verb: "Here's the recommended cut." "We'll cut this whole scene."

Cut: (Editing) Noun: "The editor screened his first cut of the film." Verb: To EDIT the film. To physically sever the film with an EDITING BLOCK or editor's scissors. To "make a cut." To go directly from one shot to another, without DISSOLVES, FLIPS, WIPES or superimpositions.

Cutaway Shots: Insert shots, extreme CLOSE-UP SHOTS, LISTENING SHOTS, AMBIENCE shots, as well as shots from another scene used as a cross-cutting scene. Shots allowing the DIRECTOR and editor to "cut away" from the main scene and add additional CHARACTER-IZATION or information; to build dramatic tension, suspense, etc.

Cutter: 1. In film editing, this is the person responsible for assembling the raw material of a film into a coherent whole. The cutter progresses gradually from an ASSEMBLY to a ROUGH CUT and then to a FINE CUT, usually deputizing the preparation of music and SOUND EFFECTS tracks to a sound cutter. The terms cutter and editor are synonymous. 2. In lighting, advice to cut down light by blocking part of the lamp with a FLAG, a CUCALORIS, a SCRIM, a BARN DOOR, etc.

Cutting Room: A room in which the positive cutting or editing (see EDIT) of films is carried out.

Cyan: LAB term for the color blue-green.

Cycle Animation: The repeated use of a set of animation cels, used for repetitive actions such as walking, traffic flow or water passing by in a river or ocean.

Cyclorama (Cyc): White or blue smooth plastic or painted wall background used to simulate limbo (see LIMBO SET) or sky. Placed at one end or curving at one corner of a sound or insert stage. A *covered cyc* is one that is gently curved at the bottom edge and can be painted to blend wall and floor with no apparent seam.

D

Dailies: The prints delivered daily from the laboratory of film materials shot on the preceding day. Now applied to all generic taped material to be utilized. Also called RUSHES.

Dance-Drama: A dramatic form of dance-storytelling utilizing other elements than dance; for example, singing, DIALOGUE, or mime. Used often in MUSICAL COMEDY and in television "production numbers."

Dance-Pantomime: A narrative dance form utilizing a blend of mime and dance.

Dancer: Performer—whether chorus or principal—whose activities in a given production are primarily dance or dance-oriented. If playing a straight role, with no dance, the dancer is then referred to as an ACTOR.

Day: SCRIPT indication giving the time of a dramatic, usually shown as "day" or "night." "Sunrise" and "dusk" are occasionally used. Example: Ext: "An open field on the edge of town—day." Or: "Night. A city street, a main thoroughfare with heavy traffic."

Day-for-Night: Filming in daylight but with special FILTERS and EXPOSURES to give a "nighttime" look; often augmented by special developing in the lab.

Daylight Conversion Filter: Used to alter the color temperature of the light coming through the LENS and striking the unexposed film that is set for artificial lighting. Also used for filming outdoors in daylight.

Daylight Loading: Full-flanged metal spool for the FILM STOCK, to protect it from being exposed to light while the camera is being loaded or unloaded.

Day Player: An ACTOR with DIALOGUE hired for or by the day, with no weekly or run-of-the-picture contract. Sometimes referred to as a BIT player. However, a day player may have a full and key scene in the picture and be further categorized as a FEATURE PLAYER.

Dead: Acoustical terminology referring to a "dry" sound with minimal reverberation, as in a recording studio.

Deadpan: A type of expressionless acting, with the face registering minimal or no emotion.

Dead Sync: In sync on the editing machine and on the interlock projector, prior to going to a COMPOSITE PRINT.

Decibel: A unit of sound measurement that increases exponentially by ten (deci-) and is named after inventor Alexander Graham Bell (-bel).

Décor: SET furnishings used to dress a scene. Furnishings and decorations for the set are selected and placed by the ART DIRECTOR and his or her staff.

Deep-Field Cinematography: A manner of filming in which both FOREGROUND and BACKGROUND settings and actions are in FOCUS. This is accomplished with small f-stops and/or lenses with short FOCAL LENGTHS.

Definition: Sharpness and clarity of a photographed image. Authenticity of reproduction of picture or sound. In sound, this would mean a high signal-level with minimal NOISE.

Defocus: For a focused image to go deliberately out of focus; used as a transition device. Also called RACK FOCUS. Lenses that are longer than normal are used for this effect.

Degauss: To electromagnetically erase the existing signal on a tape and to realign and straighten the magnetic polarities.

Demagnetize: To overcome undesirable magnetic fields by degaussing (see DEGAUSS), cleaning or coating on tape recording units, especially recording heads.

Departments: In a TV or major motion picture studio or large independent studio, the various divisions of the CREW into distinct segments and physical areas. Often the divisions are indicated by separate UNIONS: cameramen, editors, directors, etc. Generally, there is a department head and an assistant who supervise these divisions, and often handle the hiring directly. There are MAKEUP, music, sound, etc., departments.

Depolarizer: In optics, a device for eliminating the polarization of a polarized ray of light, that is, for restoring the vibrations of the ray in all directions at right angles to the ray itself. Commonly used to photograph through glass that is reflecting sun or other light so that the contents behind the glass can be seen, and also for eliminating glare from highly polished surfaces.

Depth of Field: The range of object-distances within which objects are in satisfactorily sharp FOCUS.

Depth of Focus: The range through which the image plane (emulsion surface of film) can be moved backward and forward with respect to the camera LENS, as defined under DEPTH OF FIELD. The term depth of focus is often used colloquially when depth of field is meant.

Desaturation: The elimination of color in general, or of one specific tonality, to give a monochromatic effect within a scene.

Desilu: A group of studios and enterprises set up by Desi Arnaz and Lucille Ball—whose names formed the basis for the compound word—primarily to handle the production and syndication of the *I Love Lucy* show and the *Lucy Show*, and later on, other specials and co-productions.

Detail Shot: Shots of parts of a person or his or her apparel, a dial of a TV set, an extreme close shot of the hands of a clock—all these are detail shots. A CUTAWAY is often a detail shot. In brief, a detail shot is one of either an object that is small or a small section of a larger object.

Dialogue: In a dramatic work, the exchange of conversation between two or more characters. (See also MONOLOGUE)

Dialogue Coach: A member of the production staff whose responsibility is to run the lines with the actors—usually without giving any interpretative comment—to make sure the DIALOGUE is correct before the scene is filmed or taped.

Dialogue Replacement: Replacing bad-quality sound, often from LOCATION shooting, with recording-studio quality. The actors have to be able to LIP SYNC their own voices, often from playback through earphones. Or the actors may be replacing other actors' lines, using this same technique. (See also LOOPING)

Diaphragm, Lens: An adjustable opening formed by thin overlapping plates, usually placed between the elements of the camera LENS to alter the amount of light reaching the film. Also called an *iris* because its action resembles the iris of the eye.

Dichroic Filters: Blue glass or gelatin color-balanced diffusers mounted in front of the light source to reflect excessive red and pass the blue end of the spectrum. Used for balancing an indoor-outdoor light mix, in conjunction with a #85 filter.

Diffused Light: Light that is spread out, either by atmospheric conditions, or artificially by diffusion materials. It has a certain softness to its shadows and an unconcentrated luminescence, giving a general ambience rather than bright surfaces of light.

Diffusers: Pieces of cellular diffusing composition placed in front of studio LAMPS to soften the light. Also called GELS.

Diffusion Curtain: Plastic DIFFUSER to spread light. Its origin was a plain shower curtain.

Diffusion Materials: Various plastics, silks and spun glass, used in front of the LAMPS for softening light without adding color.

Digital Video Effects: Special graphics and SPECIAL EFFECTS produced by programmed computer-control unit and checked visually before finalizing them by putting master tape on hold or making a tape-to-tape or tape-to-film copy.

Dimmer: Electrical or electromechanical device to lower or raise the amount of light in a scene. Not generally used in dramatic color photography because the voltage change also alters the color temperature of the LAMPS.

Dimmer Banks: Banks of rheostats (variable resistances) used to adjust the voltage and thus the light intensity of lamps connected to them.

DIN: A European film-exposure index referent. DIN is the acronym for *Deutsche Industrie Norm*.

Diode Tube: A tube for evacuated air with cathode and anode elements used in radio and TV receivers. Most of these have been replaced by solid-state semiconductors. One of the basic inventions making possible the effective reception of radio and TV signals.

Diopter: An extension or attachment for the LENS, which allows filming extreme CLOSE-UP material with sharp definition.

Direct Cinema: Term popularized by filmmaker Albert Maysles to describe "close-observation" shooting with indigenous sound, filmed and recorded with lightweight equipment so as to interfere minimally with the actual event.

Direction: 1. By the DIRECTOR. The input of interpretation, BLOCKING, general scenic intent, etc., given by the director to the actor or actress. The direction may be as minimal as showing the person his or her MARKS to going into a full probe of character development, motivation and subtext. 2. By the writer. The SCRIPT indications describing the actors' movements and attitudes, designated in two basic categories: GENERAL DIRECTION and personal direction. General directions are nonpersonal ones relating to one or more actors: "The young couple pauses for a moment at the doorway, then leaves." John takes the book from the desk, glances at it curiously and puts it into his traveling bag." "The horses break loose, Marie runs after them, trying to stop them." "General Stuart enters. The men stand at attention." Personal directions sometimes indicate directions to a single actor or actress but more often refer to directions included within the person's speeches, to indicate his or her mood, awareness, and, sometimes, movements.

Directional: When applied to certain optical and acoustic devices like loudspeakers, EXPOSURE METERS and microphones, this term denotes a limitation of the angle of dissemination, reflection radiation or acceptance.

Director: The person who controls the action and DIALOGUE in front of the camera and who is therefore responsible for realizing the intentions of the PRODUCER through the medium of the SHOOTING SCRIPT.

Direct-to-Disk: Recording straight to a master record rather than to a tape that can be reedited later. The advantage is an estimated higher level of recorded PRESENCE obtained by cutting out the intermediary step of tape-to-master-disk transfer and going instead directly from the master to the pressed disks. Some critics feel it gives a greater intensity by having an uninterrupted sound-take.

Dirty Dupe: A film print made directly from another print, used for editing and mixing purposes.

Discontinuity: Consecutive shots of scenes that do not match in action, DÉCOR, PROPS or LIGHTING, or any combination of these. A JUMP CUT is an example of discontinuity.

Discovery Shot: See REVEAL SHOT.

Dish: Nickname for the large parabolic antennae that receive and retransmit images to TV sets.

Dissolve: An optical impression between two superimposed shots on the screen, in which the second shot gradually begins to appear, the first shot at the same time gradually disappearing. Called *mixes* in England. (See also LAP DISSOLVE)

Dissolve Control: A special MULTIMEDIA unit that interlinks CAR-OUSEL projectors in order to DISSOLVE from one picture/slide to another.

Dissolve Lapse: Shots of brief duration filmed at spaced time-intervals and linked together with fast DISSOLVES. Similar to TIME LAPSE in its effect.

Distortion: 1. *Picture distortion* is warped and incorrect image caused by optical-system malfunction in the camera. 2. *Sound distortion* is signal malfunction between input and output of an electrical amplification or transmission system.

Documentary: 1. A type of film marked by its interpretative handling of realistic subjects and backgrounds. Sometimes the term is applied so widely as to include all films that appear more realistic than conventional COMMERCIAL pictures; sometimes so narrowly that only short films with a NARRATION and a background of real life are included. 2. According to John Grierson, one of the founders of Contemporary Documentary Film, it is "The creative treatment of reality." Documentary has developed into various styles and overlaps many other film and other tape areas—news special events, travel, biography, etc. Fiction films themselves—as well as commercials—have incorporated documentary techniques, as has documentary incorporated various techniques from many film and tape forms.

Dolby Sound: Sound system with minimal NOISE level, either on optical track or tape. This noise reduction allows for cleaner recording and greater fidelity.

Dolly: A light and compact wheeled mount for a camera, often used by small units for making DOLLYING shots and for moving a camera from place to place on set. Also, "to dolly." (See also BOOM, CAMERA, VELOCILATOR)

Dollying: Movement of the whole camera when making a shot. Sometimes referred to as trucking or tracking.

Dope Sheet: An analysis of film material prepared for purposes of library classification.

Double Exposure: Successive exposure of a light-sensitive emulsion to two scenes, so that two superimposed images are visible after development.

Double Feature: Two films on one theater program for single admission price.

Double-System Sound Recording: A method of sound recording in which the sound is originally recorded on a separate piece of film from that which records the picture image. (See also SINGLE SYSTEM sound)

Down Shot: A filmed/taped shot or scene made from a high angle.

Dream Mode: Scenes indicating the dreams or imaginings of one of the characters in the film/tape.

Dress Extra: An EXTRA who provides his or her own formal wear or special costuming and gets an additional fee for supplying them.

Drive, Camera: The mechanism through which motion is conveyed from the motor to the film in a motion picture camera.

Drive-on Pass: A studio pass allowing a vehicle to enter the motion picture lot. (See also GATE PASS)

Drop-out: A sudden total lack of recorded-sound presence, caused either by electronic malfunction or intentionally by dialing-down the sound; or by inserting blank leader. The important thing to know is that all drop-outs must be corrected and filled in with AMBIENCE, SOUND EFFECTS tracks, music or DIALOGUE, or a mixture of any or all of these.

Drop Shadow: A simulated cast shadow, usually on a lower angle than the object or lettering casting the shadow. Used often graphically in lettering so that TITLES or CREDITS stand out more distinctly.

Dub (Dubbing): 1. Synchronization with the lip movement of an actor of a voice not originally recorded in synch with the picture. The voice may or may not be that of the original actor, and it may or may not be in the same language. Dubbing is usually accomplished by means of LOOPS, consisting of short sections of the DIALOGUE that is to be replaced. Dubbing is used to record songs, prepare foreign versions of film and replace unsatisfactory dialogue. 2. Same as RE-RECORD-

ING, ELR (Electronic Line Replacement), DLR (Direct Line Replacement), LOOPING.

Dubbing Sheets: The "scoring" sheets for the DUB or MIX, which indicate in parallel columns what sounds—music, voice, effects—are on each track and at what footage they come in. Used by the MIXER(s) to cue in the necessary tracks from the mixing board.

Dulling Spray: An antireflective spray, applied to high-gloss surfaces to reduce their reflectance and cut down the highlights.

Dupe Negative: A NEGATIVE film produced by printing from a positive.

Dutch Angle: A tilted image, toward either screen left or right, effected by moving the camera from its vertical and horizontal axis and tilting it to the angle desired.

Duvatyne: A fabric that is napped and is used for covering scenery, or, in black, as background cloth for shooting scenery or people "in limbo." (See also LIMBO SET)

DVE: The abbreviation for DIGITAL VIDEO EFFECTS.

Dynalens: Gyro-controlled stabilizer that can be attached to a camera to cut down vibration and smooth out jerky or bumpy camera moves. Particularly useful in car-to-car, air-to-air and telephoto movies.

Dynamic Cutting: A term used in film aesthetics to mean a type of cutting which, by the juxtaposition of contrasting shots or SEQUENCES, generates concepts or reactions in the mind of the spectator that were not latent in any of the single elements of the film. This is thematic editing with recurring shots to structure the overall film/tape segment. No visually continuous action, but great use of visual metaphor, dramatic contrast and analogy.

Dynamic Range: The sound spread in amplitude from the softest to the loudest. Used in relation to sound recording from whatever source.

E

Easel: Graphics stand to hold title cards, charts, drawings, LOGOS, etc., for filming or taping.

East: The right side of an ANIMATION TABLE. Left is west, above is north and below is south.

Echo Chamber: A term that originated in radio. It signified a special room that had an intense reverberation-presence, giving words spoken—or sung—added power and impact used for flashback or otherworldly voices, or to enrich the narrator's voice. In singing it was utilized to give fullness to a solo voice and/or separate it from its background—a vocal chorus and/or orchestra. The echo chamber was always a separate channel fed into the MIXING BOARD. The *echo mike* often worked in an isolation booth and sometimes in a separate studio. The *echo effect* is now standard input on many contemporary instrumental and vocal recordings.

Edge Fogging: FOGGING along the edge of a piece of film, often caused by light leakage in a MAGAZINE or by inadequate taping of the lid of a film can.

Edge Number: One of a series of numbers, combined with key lettering, printed at regular intervals along the edge of many types of RAW STOCK. These numbers, incorporated in the film, print through to positive stock not so marked. The same as *footage number, key number* and *negative number*.

Edit: To arrange and assemble film or tape, prepare it for projection by INTERLOCK SYSTEM or PLAYBACK, and set it up for final sound mix.

Editing Block: A flat, solid, rectangular device with film-width grooves, used to cut FILM STOCK with a precision slice in order to re-cement or retape it to another similar cut piece of film. Sometimes a SPLICER is referred to as an editing block. Editorial process: The full range of everything needed—crew services, supplies, etc.—to assemble, fine-cut and prepare picture and tracks for the mix.

Edit Out: To take out sections of SOUND TRACK or picture.

Educational Film: Film designed primarily for classroom use. A film for inculcating concepts, attitudes and approaches to applied skills. A film of facts and information. In a nonschool context this sort of film is called an INFORMATIONAL or *motivational* film, depending on its intent.

Effect: A term that by its context refers to sound, music or OPTICAL EFFECTS. "Effects" is often indicated "FX."

Effects Filter: An optical filter that distorts the rendering of natural objects to such an extent that a special effect such as light at night or fog effect is produced.

Effects Track: A separate track for SOUND EFFECTS. There may be more than one track for sound effects—as many as two dozen on large productions utilizing numerous sounds. The SOUND TRACK is differentiated in editing and MIXING from music, narration and dialogue tracks.

Electrical Truck: Specially rigged hauling and utility truck for lights, cables and other electrical equipment. Some trucks are equipped with self-housed generators or attachments to haul and connect to generators.

Electrician: Person responsible for placement and adjustment of lights and for the supply of electricity to them. (See also GAFFER)

Electronic News-Gathering (ENG): On-the-spot news coverage utilizing videotaping systems in place of motion picture cameras. Although some stations still use films for covering news events, it is rapidly being replaced by VIDEOTAPE.

Elements: Units of original edited reversal or negative film, as well as SOUND TRACKS that are used to make the COMPOSITE PRINT.

Elements, Lens: The individual LENSES (either separate or cemented together) that in combination form a photographic objective corrected for ABERRATIONS. Lens elements are also called *components*.

ELR (Electronic Line Replacement): Film-looping process in which lines are re-recorded to match the existing synch-movement of the actor's lips, i.e., LIP SYNCH. ELR is the name for the entire session. ADR is the name for this function on videotape. (See also LOOPING, DIALOGUE REPLACEMENT)

Emmy: The name of TV's OSCAR. The Emmy awards are chosen by the Academy of Television Arts and Sciences.

Emphasis: Dramatic stress achieved in many ways—by an actor's highlighting of words in a sentence, by a gesture, by a sudden lift in volume or acceleration of tempo in the music, or through special sound or visual effects, or punctuated editorial rhythm.

Emulsion Number: A three-digit number on a RAW STOCK film container and/or can, immediately following the numerical film code number. Example: #7247, plus the three-digit number, plus closing numbers to indicate base stock.

End Sync Marks: Synchronizing marks placed at the end of reels of sound and picture film, usually to enable printing to be effected in both directions. End sync marks can also be usefully applied to recording SOUND TRACKS.

End Title(s): Closing CREDITS and/or card(s) that are run at the conclusion of a film or tape.

ENG: See ELECTRONIC NEWS-GATHERING.

Entrance: 1. The emergence of an actor or actors upon the scene. The entrance may be highlighted and set up with crescendoing anticipation; it may be unexpected, even surreptitious. But once onstage or in front of the camera, the actor has "made his or her entrance." 2. The physical location from which the actor enters.

Environmental Sound (Presence, Ambience): Actual background sounds recorded within the filming or taping of a scene: traffic, ocean roar, crowd cheering, etc. These low-level sounds can either be general sounds to LAY IN to the picture or they can be recorded and used synchronously.

Epic Film: A big film about a hero, usually larger than life, sometimes semilegendary or folkloric. It is generally a long film with numerous episodes taking place in various locales.

Equalizer: In recording, the equalizer is a device for balancing music, NARRATION, DIALOGUE and SOUND-EFFECTS tracks in a sound-mix session. This is done by altering the frequency characteristics of the electrical circuit.

Equalizing: The act of recording the various SOUND TRACKS with an EQUALIZER.

Equity: Actor's Equity Association is the full name for Equity, the UNION for stage performers. Other interlocking unions are AGMA (American Guild of Musical Artists) and AGVA (American Guild of Variety Artists).

Establishing Shot: Traditionally, a wide shot introducing locale, weather conditions (if relevant), and the introductory or complete action. The establishing shot can sometimes serve as the MASTER SHOT if it runs for the length of the complete SCENE. However, an establishing shot may be a CLOSE SHOT or MEDIUM SHOT, depending upon dramatic necessity.

ETV: Educational Television. The original name for PBS (Public Broadcasting Service). It was changed, for one reason, to lose the audience-alienating word "educational." It was also felt that the word public would make it seem more accessible.

Exciter Lamp: A lamp that "excites" a current in a PHOTOTUBE is called an exciter lamp. Often the lamp output is modulated by placing a light modulator, such as a SOUND TRACK, between the lamp and the tube.

Executive Producer: Producer in charge of the logistics of PRODUCTION. At the major lots this is often a staff producer working for the studio, and keeping track of schedules, BUDGETS and all general production areas. Sometimes this is a credit given to the person or persons whose basic contribution is obtaining production funding.

Executive Secretary: Secretary and often assistant to a PRODUCER, DIRECTOR or department head. Often in charge of the other secretaries working on a specific production.

Exit: To leave the stage and or the shot. To "make an exit." Also, the location at which the actor or actors leave.

Experimental Film: A subjective work of the FILMMAKER, using new techniques or old techniques in a new film manner. A film made independently as a personal statement.

Exploitation Film: A feature motion picture with obligatory sex, violence, horror, catastrophic events, or a mixture of any or all of these elements. It uses and openly advertises these elements to attract audiences.

Exposure: Exposing a photographic film to any given intensity of light in such a manner that it may produce a latent image on the emulsion. According to the reciprocity law, exposure is determined by the product of time and intensity of illumination. *Overexposure* is an exposure greater than optimum for a particular photographic emulsion, developing condition and range brightness. *Underexposure* is an exposure less than the optimum for a particular photographic emulsion.

Exposure Index: A number based on emulsion speed and latitude, EXPOSURE METER characteristics and technique, and expected conditions of development, which enables the user of a film emulsion to determine the correct exposure under different light conditions, estimated by an exposure meter or from tables.

Exposure Meter: A device for determining the light flux incident upon or reflected from a scene to be photographed, the corresponding instruments being known as *incident-light meters* and *reflected-light meters*. The most common type in use in motion picture photography is that on which the user notes the reading on a calibrated microammeter actuated by a photovoltaic cell.

Ext: The abbreviation for EXTERIOR.

Exterior: Outdoor scene.

Extra: A film supernumerary, ATMOSPHERE, BACKGROUND. There are UNION and nonunion extras. Their most effective union is SEG, Screen Extras Guild. SEG pay is less than SAG, and unless specifically contracted, SEG members receive no residuals.

Extreme: SCRIPT designation used in terms such as "extreme CU," "extreme LONG SHOT," or "extreme LOW ANGLE." It is abbreviated with an "E" or an "X": XCU or ECU means "extreme CLOSE-UP."

Eye-Level: The standard head-on height of any shot, establishing people or places. Roughly five and one-half feet from the floor base to the lens opening.

F

Fade: 1. An OPTICAL EFFECT occupying a single shot, in which the shot gradually disappears into blackness (FADE-OUT) or appears out of blackness (FADE-IN). The most usual convention for this is to note the passage of time as opposed to the DISSOLVE, which usually notes related or continuous action of longer intervals than a CUT. 2. To come from or go into black from the pictorial image.

Fade-in: To start from black or a color wash and let the picture fade into full delineated image.

Fade-out: When the vanishing image goes into black or into—as in a FADE-IN—a color wash.

Fall-off: The diminution of the amount of light in increasing distance from its direct source. Light from a given position drops off as the square of the distance.

Fan: An avid follower and admirer of media (see MEDIUM) performers.

Fanfare: A musical flourish—usually on brass, sometimes accompanied by percussion—to open a drama or an important/regal scene within the work. Example of fanfare used on TV would be Masterpiece Theatre's "Fanfare for Trumpet" by Jean Joseph Mouret.

Fast Film: Film with an American Standards Association rating of 100 or more, giving it greater sensitivity to light.

Fast Lens: A lens with an f-value of 2.8 or faster; "faster" in this case meaning a lower number on the scale: 1.2, .09, etc.

Fast Motion: Motion of the film through the camera slower than the standard speed, which therefore results in action appearing faster than normal when the film is projected at the standard rate. (See also SLOW MOTION)

Favor: To give scenic dominance to a performer. (See also FEATURE, Verb, 2)

FCC: See FEDERAL TRADE COMMISSION.

Feature: Noun: A full-length dramatic film, made for theatrical release. Feature-length made-for-television films or tapes are often referred to as *TV films, Movies-of-the-Week, TV specials,* etc. Verb: 1. To give billing to a performer just below that of the leading STARS. To give him or her prominence. 2. To concentrate on a particular performer in a scene; to favor, by lighting or placement.

Feature Length: Seventy minutes, plus. Although few features today run less than 90 minutes. Under rules of the ACADEMY OF MOTION PICTURE ARTS AND SCIENCES, a "feature DOCUMENTARY" length is 30 minutes or more.

Feature Player: Principal performer in a film or TV show. Supporting players to the STARS. Today's feature player CREDITS, however, may read in a list headed with the words "Also starring . . ."

Featuring: "It was a low-budget film, featuring all unknown actors." "It was a big musical, featuring extravaganza numbers, set against minimal plot."

Federal Trade Commission (FCC): U.S. government organization set up for the purposes of preventing misrepresentation and fraud in advertising, and to investigate and curb monopolies. In both radio and TV, it has forced less-than-truthful claims by sponsors to be brought into closer proximity to the truth. Its truth-in-packaging has brought about many changes in the way products are filmed/taped for TV commercials, and/or in the text accompanying the product.

Feed Lines: The delivery by an actor of his or her lines from OFF-CAMERA position for the benefit of the on-camera actor. The lines are delivered to cue in the on-camera actor or to give the on-camera DIALOGUE to which he or she can react.

FG: The abbreviation for FOREGROUND.

Fidelity: Authenticity of sound or picture.

Field (Action Field): Physical portion of the scene that is framed (see FRAMING) for filming/taping.

Field Camera: DOCUMENTARY news and general location camera. Easily portable because of its light weight and simple carry-design.

Field Chart: A transparent acetate guide with concentric rectangles indicating areas covered by gradations of camera positions. It is mounted onto an animation table or plate by pegs that are premeasured to match peg holes on the acetate sheet.

Fill Leader: LEADER laid in to an editing reel to indicate where a shot or scene is to be. Or a temporary film repair of the same FRAME length of the replaced damaged SCENE. The same term applies to sound as well as picture.

Fill Light: The light that builds up shadow illumination. The ratio of KEY LIGHT to fill light establishes in general terms the lighting contrast of a SCENE.

Film: A thin flexible ribbon of transparent material having perforations along one or both edges and bearing a sensitized layer or other coating capable of producing photographic images.

Film Archive: A reference library of film, to be used for research and/or STOCK FOOTAGE in DOCUMENTARY or documentary-type films. (An example of the latter would be a staged documentary such as an historical re-creation.) Film archives may also contain printed materials, posters, magazines and clippings relating to these films.

Film Chain: Electromechanical hookup projecting film into a television system.

Film Clip: A small portion of film from a longer motion picture, used, for example, in films on motion picture history. Also used in assembling a preview of coming attractions.

Film Continuity: The straight-through flow of action that is "filmically" correct: proper direction of movements of camera or on-camera subjects; proper matching of picture and sound from one shot to another; proper rhythm of FADES, DISSOLVES, and CUTS; correct script text; clear visual and auditory delineation of the film's intended theme(s).

Film Exchanges: Regional centers from which films are distributed to individual movie theaters.

Film Festival: A special commercial, social and cultural event featuring the showings of numerous and varied types of films. It ordinarily takes place in one city over a period of several days and is climaxed by the presentation of commendations, awards and prizes.

Film-Footage Table: A conversion table equating 35mm and 16mm footage to time, and vice versa.

Film Gate: A camera or projector device consisting of combined PRESSURE PLATES and APERTURE PLATES that guide film past and maintain proper focal distance between film and LENS.

Film Gauge: Standard width of basic motion picture FILM STOCKS.

Filmic: Those dramatic, technical and directorial elements found primarily—or only—in film.

Filmic Space: The aesthetic power of the film medium that enables it to combine shots of widely disparate origins into a single framework of space.

Filmic Time/Space: Most film sequences deal with compressed time, with the exception of SLOW-MOTION segments or something as detailed and expanded in time as the celebrated Odessa steps sequence in *Potemkin*. Transposition of time through compression, extension, FLASHBACKS and FLASH-FORWARDS are all examples of filmic time. Movement in space can be accomplished with a direct CUT—Moscow to Paris—almost instantaneously. Then, too, outer space can be simulated and "travel" through it speeded up or slowed down as necessary. The connection between otherwise disparate shots can sometimes be delineated by either a linking musical leit-motif or a SECOND EFFECT.

Film Library: The organization of the film material in possession of a studio, correlated by means of a reference and/or cross-index system.

Film Loader: The member of a camera team whose function is to load unexposed film into MAGAZINES and unload exposed film into cans. Except in a very large unit, the functions of a loader are dis-charged by an assistant cameraman.

Film Loop: 1. Lengths of FILM or SOUND TRACK SPLICED end-to-end to form a continuous loop for PLAYBACK, used in LOOPING and DIA-LOGUE REPLACEMENT sessions. 2. A piece of master or original film run through a printer for multiple copies. 3. A continuous loop of completed film (music, EFFECTS, DIALOGUE and NARRATION) on a special cartridge for projection. 4. Slack film—on projectors and cam-eras—between SPROCKET rollers and the DRIVE and TAKE-UP mech-anisms.

Film Magazine: Detachable lightproof container for holding FILM STOCK as it passes through the camera. One compartment of the magazine is for the virgin film stock; the other chamber is the take-up side for the exposed footage.

Filmmaker: A person who directly and individually handles and/or supervises all of the production steps necessary to create and pro-duce a complete film.

Film Noir: Films whose story lines are built on "dark" characters—thieves, con men, prostitutes, paid killers, gamblers, night people—who are portrayed, often violently, in situations of high action and confrontation. Also called *cinema noir, black cinema*.

Film Ratio: Number of feet of film shot in direct relation to number of feet used in the running length of the film. A FEATURE that runs 90 minutes has a production footage of 90 minutes times 90 feet per minute, or 8100 feet. (This does not include head and tail LEADERS.)

To get that final 8100, as much 81,000 feet might have been shot, making the film ratio 10-to-1. DOCUMENTARIES, because of their un- predictable nature, may run a higher footage ratio. They are mostly shot in 16mm (36 feet per minute), so that a final footage count for film shot for a 54-minute film (1944 feet, excluding leaders) might be 41,000 feet. That would result in a film ratio of approximately 21-to- 1. Some segments of the Jacques Cousteau underwater specials for TV had as high as a 200-to-1 film ratio. A term used by camer- amen, editors and lab technicians to describe film ratio is *footage- shot-to-footage-used*.

Film Running Speed: Movement rate of film through a camera or projector, indicated in FRAMES PER SECOND (FPS), or in feet/meters per minute.

Film Stock: Unexposed and unprocessed rolls of film. Standard roll- lengths are 100′, 200′, 400′, 1000′ and 2000′. Called, before ex- posed, *virgin stock*.

Film Storage: Filmkeeping in vaults that are humidity and temper- ature controlled. Storage for original footage, including elements, OUTS, FINE-GRAIN masters, SOUND TRACKS, etc. Film is "vaulted" when not in active postproduction use.

Filmstrip: A series of STILL pictures, printed sequentially, to be viewed one FRAME at a time. Printed and projected on 8mm, 16mm or 35mm stock. Used mainly for instructional and motivational purposes.

Film Structure: The architectonics of the conceptual skeleton that holds a film together: PLOT, CHARACTERIZATION, recurring motif, time progression, etc.

Filter: 1. Optical unit for the camera's LENS system, made to absorb specific elements of the incoming light spectra. 2. A *sound filter* is designed to thin out preselected narrow-frequency bands.

Filter Factor: A numerical factor by which the length of a photo- graphic exposure must be increased to compensate for the absorp- tion of an optical filter through which the exposure is to be made.

Filter Holder: A term for any slot, frame or attachment that holds the necessary filters in front of the camera LENS during filming.

Filter Mike: A microphone with low-reverberatory frequencies minimized, giving a flat, slightly nasal sound. Used to simulate voices coming over a public loudspeaker, intercom or phone receiver.

Filters (Optical): 1. *Black and White:* The basic uses of filters when shooting in black and white are for making the sky appear darker or for cutting through overcast or hazy weather. The filter intensifies its own color, making it darker, resulting in lighter tones in the complementary range. Today, however, the minimal amount of "black and white" filming is often done in color and printed in black and white. 2. *Color:* Good color can be brought to its optimum only by correct filtering, by using the proper lighting to match the preset color balance of the FILM STOCK. 3. *Daylight:* The #85 is the "daylight" workhorse. It can be used in conjunction with high-speed film by utilizing an ND .30 (neutral density) filter. 4. *Diffusion:* Diffusion filters are for taking the hard edge-lines off camera subjects, people or products. These softening filters should be used judiciously, so that they can intercut effectively with the nondiffuse footage. 5. *Fog:* A special type of DIFFUSION FILTER available in a widely varying scale, with a different effect for each filter. Tests are recommended before production filming commences. 6. *Neutral density:* A gray filter that reduces the light striking the lens. It is an omnicolor lens, maintaining color balance naturally, as it affects all colors equally. Therefore, neutral density filters do not change the color balance, but cut off light, allowing increase in the lens aperture, and lowering CONTRAST. 7. *Polarizing:* Filter used with sunlight or reflections on glass and water. This controls or eliminates unwanted reflection. The desired effects of the polarization filtering must be determined by viewing through the finder while rotating the filter. 8. *Protection:* Prime quality clear glass mounted in a filter holder to keep dust, snow, rain, etc., away from the lens.

Final Cut: The last fine-tuning immediately following acceptance of FINE CUT, wherein the sound is mixed and the picture conformed and made ready for the lab to run off the FIRST-ANSWER PRINT.

Finder: See VIEWFINDER.

Fine Cut: The version of the WORKPRINT of a film that follows the ROUGH-CUT stage in the film's progress. At each successive stage, the cutting is refined and unnecessary FOOTAGE eliminated.

Fine-Grain: The term used to designate film emulsions in which the GRAIN size is smaller or finer than the older type emulsions commonly employed prior to about 1936. Fine-grain film is usually slower (requiring more exposure) than other films.

Fine-Grain Dupe: 1. DUPE NEGATIVE from a MASTER POSITIVE, taken from the original black and white negative. 2. Dupe negative made directly from contact reversal-printing process from the original black and white negative.

Fine-Grain Master Positive: Next processing step (in black and white) that comes after the original black and white NEGATIVE. This both protects the ORIGINAL and allows printing of OPTICAL EFFECTS.

First-Answer Print: First conformed and sound-mixed COMPOSITE print from the lab. It is this print that is checked by the lab timer and producer for color timings, sound-printing and synchronization to see if they are correct and satisfactory.

First-Generation Dupe: A reversal print made from a reversal-stock original or master tape, often for the purpose of producing further prints or tapes, which are known as *second-generation dupes*.

First Run: The premiere cycle of the exhibition of a film.

Fisheye Lens: Extreme WIDE-ANGLE LENS.

Fishpole: A lightweight rod or pole on which a microphone is mounted. It is hand-held by one of the sound crew during shooting.

Flack: 1. A press agent. 2. The material planted by a press agent: notices, stories, special articles, photos with captions, etc. 3. All news releases in all media (see MEDIUM) referring to clients of the press agent.

Flag: A miniature GOBO, made of plywood or of cloth mounted on a metal frame and usually set on a stand. (See also SCRIM)

Flange: A disk, usually made of metal or plastic, against which film, mounted on a rewinder, is wound on a CORE.

Flares: Areas of highlight intensity in the NEGATIVE film image, caused by internal reflections in the camera lens or by starry reflections from bright objects in the camera.

Flashback: A scene or full sequence looking backward in time from the dramatic "present action." Some films, such as John Huston's classic *The Man Who Would Be King* have only a few opening and closing scenes, and the entire balance of the film is told in flashback. *Flashback action* refers to those things that happened before the film's "present" time reference.

Flash-Forward: Anticipatory shot or scene, indicating future action yet to happen in the film. Also called *flash-ahead*.

Flash Frame: One FRAME inserted within a specific shot to give a rapid, percussive image. (See also SUBLIMINAL CUT)

Flatbed: A MOVIOLA editing machine with a horizontal instead of upright working area. It consists of circular plates, one for feed-out, one for take-up. There are at least two sets of these plates—one for picture and one for sound. Other plate sets are for additional SOUND TRACKS, and, in some models, for additional picture.

Flicker: In film projection, a rate of fewer FRAMES per second than PERSISTENCE OF VISION can fuse into a continuous mental image. Also a fluctuation in the intensity of light thrown on the screen, caused by the passage of the SHUTTER across the light beam.

Flip: Optical effect in which the frame of film seems to turn on either a horizontal or vertical axis and "flip" to another image on the "other side."

Flipover Wipe: A kind of WIPE in which the image appears to turn over, revealing another image on the "back," the axis of rotation being either vertical or horizontal.

Flub: 1. For an actor or actress, a flub occurs when he or she blows a line or makes an error of movement: "Be careful this time not to flub that line!" 2. For the crew, it is any technical error during filming or FRAMING.

Fluid Head: A camera mount filled with a special viscous fluid device that gives just enough resistance to allow for smooth camera movements.

Flutter: Unwanted erratic movement in a camera causing pictorial jumps and/or unevenly exposed FRAMES, or, on a sound recorder, slurs, speed-ups or DROP-OUTS.

Fly: To suspend scenery above a SET by ropes or cables.

F Number: A number denoting the geometrical determination of LENS speed. A numerical scale based on the division of the FOCAL LENGTH of a lens by the diameter of the lens opening.

Focal Length: The constant of a LENS upon which the size of the image depends. In a thin lens, it is the distance from the center of the lens to either principal FOCUS. The equivalent focal length of a thick lens is the focal length of a thin lens of identical magnifying power.

Focal Plane: Perpendicular plane to the axis of a LENS, wherein the image is formed when the lens is focused on infinity.

Focus: The point at which parallel rays meet after passing through a convergent LENS. More generally, that position at which an object must be situated in order that the image produced by a lens may be sharp and well defined; hence an object is spoken of as *in focus* or *out of focus*.

Focusing: The art of moving a camera LENS toward or away from an emulsion plane to bring the image on this plane into FOCUS.

Focusing Microscope: An optical device in many cameras of superior design for magnifying the image formed on a GROUND GLASS by the camera LENS.

Fogging: The exposure of film to unwanted light, due to camera or MAGAZINE light-leaks or from being light-struck while loading or unloading. Fogging can also be done in the lab, either purposely by special processing or by accident from improper processing.

Fogmaker: A device that puts out controlled amounts of "cooled" smoke so that it will settle low to the ground, creating the illusion of fog, mist or smoke.

Foley: To add postproduction SOUND EFFECTS to a picture by watching the SCENE and simulating EFFECTS to match the ACTION. For example, a scene may be shot without sound of a man walking in the snow. The foleying sound-effects man will watch the scene— usually on a LOOP—and rehearse it, then go for a TAKE. The takes that match the closest are the ones selected for turning over to the editor. Foleying can be used to add sound where the scene is filmed/ taped MOS, where the sound needs to be augmented or where existing sound has to be replaced.

Foleying Session: Time and stage reserved for recording the foleyed effects.

Foleying Stage: Soundstage set up to handle foleying.

Follow Focus: A continuous change in camera FOCUSING, necessitated by relative movement between the camera and its subject, greater than can be accommodated by DEPTH OF FIELD. To follow focus is usually a function of the first assistant cameraman.

Follow Shots: Another name for DOLLYING or trucking shots. A shot in which a moving camera follows the action of a scene.

Follow Spotlight (Spots): Spotlights used where there are great light-throw distances. They work from an electric arc that radiates light between two carbons. Used in MUSICAL COMEDIES, sporting events, rock concerts, etc.

Footage: 1. Film length based on a scale of feet. The amount of film run through the camera in production. 2. The projected amount of FILM STOCK needed to cover a scene or event. Even when measured in meters it is still called footage.

Footage-Time Calculator: A linear or wheel-shaped chart giving correlations between running time and FOOTAGE for various film gauges at various speeds.

Foot Candle: A basic lighting measurement of the illumination striking a spherical surface from a distance of one foot from the light source.

Foot Candle Meter: A light meter calibrated to take its readings in FOOT CANDLES.

Foot Irons: Specially designed metallic hardware used to secure scenery to the floor.

Foreground: The action area nearest to the camera. The antonym is BACKGROUND, but the term *middle ground* is also used for shots that cover a great area, especially in depth of scene.

Format: 1. FILM-STOCK dimensions, giving the measurement of the FRAME area, perforation sizes and total area. 2. The working space or framed action area of a show to be filmed or taped. 3. The standard structure of a daily or weekly TV show.

Four-Walling: Exhibiting a film wherein the distributor pays the theater owner a preset negotiated price to cover theater costs and pro-rated theater income for a given period of time. This fee is for the use of the "four walls" of the theater. Ticket rates, promotion and advertising are at the distributor's discretion. All monies that exceed the wall-to-wall theater costs go directly to the distributor. Concession sales are negotiable.

Frame: The individual picture on film, tape or VIDEODISK.

Frames Per Second (FPS): Number of FRAMES that are exposed as they run emulsion out past the camera lens. This can also refer to PROJECTOR speed. In 16mm and 35mm, the SOUND-SPEED rate is 24 frames per second. The FOOTAGE measurement is in feet per minute: 36 feet per minute in 16mm and 90 in 35mm.

Framing: The setting up of a camera in such a way that the image framed by its LENS and APERTURE PLATE is precisely that required by the DIRECTOR and CAMERAMAN. (See also LINING UP)

Freeze Frame: A single FRAME that is re-printed as many frames as the running time of the freeze-frame shot requires. It visually stops and holds the action for accent and emphasis for whatever length of time is required. Also called *stop frame, hold frame.*

Fresnel Lens: Originally developed for utilization in lighthouse beacons. The concentric rings on the circular glass lens spread the light even more evenly. The name is derived from the French physicist Augustin Jean Fresnel. Pronounced "frah-nel."

Friction Head: A PAN-AND-TILT HEAD set on a TRIPOD or other camera support. It employs a smoothly sliding friction device to secure smoothness of camera movement.

Front Projection: A method—of which there are several—of projecting background images onto a special screen behind the actors. Compensating lighting is added to eliminate the projected image that falls on the actors.

Frosted Plate: Flat glass or plastic translucent plate coated with diffusing material.

FTC: SEE FEDERAL TRADE COMMISSION.

Full Aperture: Widest opening of the iris of a LENS.

Full Coat: Film that is magnetically coated on one side with iron oxide.

Full Shot: A shot that includes the full height of the actors, head-to-toe. It can also mean a shot that includes everything in the scene at its widest angle not included in the framing of the ESTABLISHING SHOT.

Furniture Pad: An insulated cloth pad used by moving van companies for furniture. Used in the film/tape business for many production functions: as a ground pad on which the cameraman can stretch out at ground level for a LOW-ANGLE shot, as an improvised sound baffle, as a sun shield to keep light off the camera, as a buffer for carrying delicate equipment, etc. These pads, originally obtained from moving van companies, are now manufactured to meet film needs and specifications.

Fuzzy: An image that has too soft a FOCUS or is not sharply delineated.

G

Gaffer: The chief electrician who is responsible, under the first cameraman, for the LIGHTING of SCENES.

Gaffer's Tape: All-purpose cloth or plastic adhesive tape utilized for improvised functions during production. It is often used to attach GOBOING devices to CENTURY-STAND arms or even to the body of the camera itself, or to stabilize PROPS, hold IDIOT BOARDS in place, etc.

Gang Synchronizer: The term is normally preceded by a number that tells how many SPROCKET wheels the unit has. A *three-gang synchronizer* can handle three strips of film; a *four-gang*, four; and so on. On most gang splicers there are sound heads so that SYNCHRONISM can be determined. Used for matching SOUND TRACKS to a WORKPRINT, and for matching a print to the ORIGINAL. (See also SPLICE)

Gate: 1. The APERTURE unit of cameras and projectors. 2. The gross amount of money taken in at the BOX OFFICE or on metered CLOSED-CIRCUIT or special-circuit TV on any given attraction. Originally a circus/carnival term, then applied to the legitimate theater, then to the mass media. Derived from *ticket gate*. Also called *box office*.

Gate Pass: A written pass left at the studio gate for a particular person, permitting access to the studio. Also called *walk-on pass*. (See also DRIVE-ON PASS)

Gator Clamp Lamp: A small lamp with a permanent GATOR-GRIP attached, allowing for immediate placement for lighting its particular area.

Gator Grip: A strong multipurpose metal clamp, often insulated on the clamp handles with plastic as protection against electrical shock. This alligator-type grip is used to attach foliage branches to a scenic support, lightweight lamps to furniture sets or CENTURY STANDS. It is also used to clamp sound-baffling sheets or white reflector cards into place.

Gear Head: A type of PAN-AND-TILT HEAD set on a TRIPOD or crane, which incorporates two gear-drives for the two movements, operated by crank handles.

Gel: Short for *gelatin*, the transparent or translucent plastic color pieces that fit into color frames.

General Direction: Direction in a SCRIPT—usually starting on the far left margin of the page—that describes general actions—ENTRANCES, EXITS, movements, group reactions and so forth. Opposed to *personal direction*, which pinpoints feelings, reactions, and gestures of a particular player, and are included primarily—in parentheses—within the body of the player's dramatic speeches.

Gliss: Short for *glissando*. This musical dipping and rising effect was used in dramatic radio in a similar manner to a STING. The direction *gliss sting* was not uncommon. It was musical punctuation in comedy shows as well; often followed by a crash, splash, slide whistle or explosion. The term was never widely used in TV or film scripts.

Glitch: An electronic disturbance on a tape or a misfunction on a piece of film: a SPROCKET jump, a color mismatch, a sound dropout, etc.

Glossy: A high-reflective finish on a still photo. Used for mail-outs to fans, printed reproductions and most professional photos in actors' portfolios. As opposed to MATTE FINISH.

Gloves: Cotton gloves worn by film editors and lab technicians so as not to get finger marks on original exposed film while handling it.

Gobo: 1. A wooden screen, painted black and so placed that it screens one or more studio LAMPS, thus preventing light from entering the camera lens. Usually mounted on adjustable stands, and of many shapes and sizes. 2. Any shielding device to keep light from directly striking the camera lens. Often a black-cloth-covered frame hand-held or mounted on a CENTURY STAND.

Grain: The grouping together of clusters of fine silver particles, individually too small to be seen under normal viewing conditions. This clustering can cause particles to become visually distinguishable, thereby resulting in what is described as GRAININESS.

Graininess: A photographic image in which the many individual particles are apparent when projected.

Grand Manner: A full-blown stylized way of acting, with broad gestures, mannered readings and even asides to the audience. The grand manner essays larger-than-life characterizations, playing for results and indicating dramatically important points by using strong vocal underlining. A good example of this is the film classic *Tom Jones*, or Zeffirelli's *Taming of the Shrew* and *La Traviata*.

Gravel Box: A wooden box filled with pebbles and crushed rock used for SOUND-EFFECT simulation—in FOLEYING or in radio—of a person or persons walking on gravel. Usually a standard on a FOLEYING STAGE.

Gray Scale: Gradation of "steps" in gray fields, from white to black, represented on a check chart used by labs and cameramen.

Green-Man: Man in charge of dressing the SET—interior or exterior—with greenery, both growing plants or trimmed and remounted branches and/or trunks.

Grid: A piece of studio RIGGING, consisting of interlocking metal pipes—aluminum or steel—that are suspended horizontally from the ceiling area immediately above the soundstage filming/taping area.

Grip: The person who, on the studio SET, has charge of minor adjustments and repairs the PROPS, CAMERA TRACKS and the like.

Ground Glass: A piece of glass with a finely ground surface on which an image can be formed. Used in the VIEWFINDERS of cameras. The image is often enlarged by means of a FOCUSING MICROSCOPE.

Guide: 1. A *leader's guide* is a manual for the person in charge of showing the EDUCATIONAL FILM or tape to which the guide serves as a discussion handbook. 2. A *study guide* is a booklet handed out to teachers, and sometimes to students, which augments the materials covered in the film. Can be used for study before and/or after the screening. 3. A *teacher's guide* is a pamphlet that instructs the teacher on basic and ancillary points to be derived from the film or tape. Also, it may contain a bibliography for supportive reading and/ or AUDIOVISUAL materials.

Guide-Line: An editor's marking that moves on, across and off the screen, serving as a standby and/or direct cue to the actor who is LOOPING the lines. Often the direct cue is after the line clears the FRAME.

Guild: The name for most of the performing arts *unions*: A few are: Screen Actors Guild, Directors Guild of America, American Guild of Variety Artists, American Guild of Musical Artists.

Gyro Head: A camera-mount device that is stabilized by an internal mechanism that drives a rapidly spinning flywheel. This smooths out the erratic movement of the camera, especially in shots made on a moving vehicle or HAND-HELD.

H

Hacker: Computer technician and expert programmer.

Hair Stylist: Person whose job it is to dress the hair of the on-camera performer and to maintain its appearance during the film/taping.

Halogen Lamp: One that reuses part of its own burn-off tungsten to give it longer life and a more even color temperature.

Hand Camera: Lightweight motion picture or television camera, ideal for HAND-HELD shots.

Handgrip: A special handle mount for cameras, used for making HAND-HELD shots. Also called *handhold*.

Hand-held: A shot made without benefit of TRIPOD, DOLLY or CRANE, where the camera is held by the cameraman. (See also STEADICAM)

Hand Props: Easily portable and lightweight PROPS, carried by the performer or employed in the scene. Examples would be a handgun, a box of candy, a bouquet, a telephone, a knapsack, an alarm clock.

Hard Ticket: 1. Ticket on regular ticket stock that is paid for by the holder. Not a COMP, two-for-one or press pass. 2. A paid-for reserved seat.

Hazard Pay: Additional fees over and above the daily rate for any work involving risk. A cameraman receives such pay any time he or she must film from a plane or helicopter, use a safety belt for security, or in any high-speed situation. Fees for STUNTPERSONS are hazard-fee rates, predicated totally upon degree of risk.

Head: 1. In an editing machine the VIEWER and SOUND READER. 2. In sound terminology, the sensitized optical or tape reader used for playing, or in SYNCH SOUND.

Head, Camera: 1. The revolving and tilting mount on which a camera is fixed, and which in turn is fixed to a TRIPOD, HIGH HAT, DOLLY, VELOCILATOR, or BOOM. 2. Special camera FILTER that absorbs ultraviolet light.

Head Gaffer: First electrician on a film production.

Head-on Shot: Action moving directly toward camera.

Head-out: A REEL of film so wound that the first FRAME is on the outside of the reel, ready to project. The opposite term is *tails-up* or *tails-out*. Also called *head-up*.

Heads: 1. Sound recording or PLAYBACK units, custom sensitized for such requirements. Used on sound recorders, MOVIOLAS, playback units, etc. 2. Front ends of film REELS as opposed to TAILS.

Headset: Sound-receiving unit for one or both ears that slips onto the sound technician's head, often with a mini-microphone attached.

Head Shot: A tight CLOSE-UP in which the on-camera performer's head fills the FRAME.

Heavy: The villain, the antagonist. This character in a dramatic work classically opposes the *protagonist*: the HERO or heroine.

Hero: 1. The *protagonist*. The leading character, who opposes the *antagonist*; the HEAVY; the villain. 2. The "good" car, horse, etc. The *hero product* is the sponsor's item used in a commercial and treated as the STAR.

Hi-Con (High-Contrast): 1. An image, basically black and white, with minimal gradation tones. 2. Film that is used to obtain this effect.

High Hat: A very small solid TRIPOD of fixed height that can be attached to the floor or to a movable, flat board for LOW-ANGLE shots.

High Hat: (Lighting) A metallic snoot, usually painted black, that fits over a light and cuts down the spill light, more sharply delineating the light-pool area. Also called a *funnel*.

High-Key: Infusing the action area with illumination stressing the lighter tones.

High-Key Lighting: Lighting preset to produce HIGH-KEY images.

High-Level: "Loud" sector of a given sound range.

Highlights: Within a lighted scene of action, the brightest areas of illumination, having a high level of reflectivity.

High Shot: A shot above eye level of the action, as opposed to a LOW-ANGLE shot.

High-Speed Camera: A camera that moves the film rapidly through the GATE at speeds greatly exceeding the normal FPS rate. This can be a few hundred FRAMES to thousands of frames per second. The effect of this high-speed cinematography is one of extreme SLOW MOTION when shown at normal speed. Used for product analysis, research and SPECIAL EFFECTS.

High-Speed Film: 1. FILM STOCK with added perforations, to use in high-speed cinematography. 2. Film with a high ASA (American Standards Association) rating, very sensitive to light. (See also ASA INDEX)

Hit: Noun: A successful film, TV or radio program with a good box-office take or listener-rating number. Verb: "Hit the lights!" A command to the lighting crew, given by the head GAFFER, DP or ASSISTANT DIRECTOR to turn on the lights for the scene to be shot. "Be sure to hit your marks." Direction from an AD, DP (director of photography) or DIRECTOR to an actor or camera crew to be certain to land on proper preset positional floor markings on the right word cue or countdown.

Hollywood: A vague geographical term relating roughly to the greater Los Angeles area, there being no incorporated city or mayor of Hollywood. MGM, for instance, is in Culver City; Warner's and Columbia's main shooting stages and corporate offices are in Burbank; Twentieth Century–Fox is in West Los Angeles; and Disney's complex stretches from Burbank and Glendale to West San Fernando Valley. It is a name signifying more the "image" of Hollywood than an actual place.

Hologram: A three-dimensional laser-produced image in conjunction with special photographic equipment.

Holography: Photography designed to produce HOLOGRAMS.

Honey Wagon: A portable dressing room with its own toilet(s).

Horse Opera: A Western feature film or TV segment. Also called an OATER.

Horseshoe Staging: Staging in which the audience sits in front and on both sides of the performers, often utilizing a thrust stage. Used especially for audience-participation shows, musical groups, and variety material. Developed from legitimate theater staging.

Hot Splicer: Editor's SPLICER that electrically heats the SPLICE to accelerate the holding effect of the film cement.

Hot Spot: Unwanted HIGHLIGHT caused by LIGHTING that is too strong for the given area.

Houselights: The lights within the audience areas of a theater or audience studio for filming or taping, but not those lights located or focused on the stage area proper.

House Manager: The person in charge of a live theater or movie house who runs the theater's logistics and ticket sales. Sometimes the house manager is also owner or co-owner of the "house."

How-to Film: A motion picture that explains and demonstrates a skill, mechanical process or concept.

Hue: Gradation of color.

Hype: Publicity and advertising, including personal and TV talk-show appearances, newspaper and magazine articles, etc., to promote and publicize a film or TV program and/or series.

Hyphenate: One who works in more than one PRODUCTION capacity, often with UNION cards for each function: writer-director, actor-writer, producer-director, etc.

Hypo (Hyposulfite): A solution that chemically stops the development process by lifting out undeveloped silver particles and hardening the gelatinous coating.

I

IBEW: See INTERNATIONAL BROTHERHOOD OF ELECTRICAL WORKERS.

Idiot Board: Cue cards with CUES and DIALOGUE for reference by the actor or actress. In some cases this is replaced by systems such as Q-TV, which is an electronic roll on a reflective glass plate directly in front of the camera, beveled at an angle so as to be read by the performer and not visible to the camera lens. Also called *idiot sheet*. (See also Q-TV)

Illuminaire: In broad parlance, any light source—LAMP, candle, REFLECTOR bouncing light into a scene, flashlight, SUNGUN, etc. Any unit that provides illumination. In studio use, any working lamp. Illuminaire is an international filmmaking term and is also used in glossaries and guides in communication departments in the groves of Academe.

Imaginary Line: A line thought of as passing through two or more performers. The crossing of this line results in a filmic mismatch that will not edit correctly. This mismatch is known as *crossing the line* or *false reverse*.

Imax: Super-large-screen process developed in Canada, using a special camera with a horizontal film-through-camera movement to achieve maximum image-surface. The IMAX can therefore be ten times the size of a conventional screen. Wider than Cinerama, the screen is also taller, creating an effect much more compelling than wide-screen alone. The IMAX screen measures 75 × 100.5 feet, as opposed to a standard 35mm 19 × 45-foot area or a Cinerama 70mm 31 × 64-foot screen.

Improvise: 1. For the performer(s) to invent on-the-spot DIALOGUE and/or action. 2. To work out production problems utilizing fallback or instantly devised methods.

In-Camera Matte Shot: Shot wherein a portion of the action field is masked off by a black cutout device formed to meet scenic specifications. This is placed either directly in front of the FOCAL PLANE or mounted in a MATTE BOX in front of the camera.

In Character: Correct attitudinal identification by the ACTOR or ACTRESS with the role he or she is playing. DIALOGUE or action that seems natural to the part.

Inching Knob: A turning handle that interlocks with the drive mechanism of a GANG SYNCHRONIZER or other piece of editing or projection equipment that can take the film forward or put it in reverse in accelerated or decelerated moves. These moves can be made by hand or be motor driven.

Incident Light: Light from all surrounding sources that illuminates the on-camera subject.

Independent Production: TV or film production not affiliated with a major studio. Independent productions range from full UNION to subcontracted crews to nonunion casts and crews, and mixtures of all of these.

Indigenous Sound: The real sound (matching or sync) of the LOCATION that is being filmed. Its PRESENCE. Also called *ambient sound, actual sound, presence track.*

Industrial Film: An informational, motivational or propaganda film, the subject of which is a factory, industrial group, utility or conglomerate.

Informational Film/Tape: A structured media (see MEDIUM) presentation of facts, procedures and conceptual themes.

Infrared: The region of the spectrum ranging upward from 700 millimicrons, eventually merging with heat waves. Infrared motion picture film is chiefly used for haze penetration and for producing special non-PANCHROMATIC effects.

Ingenue: A female leading role—"the young, ingenuous woman," hence, "ingenue." Age range: late teens to mid-twenties.

In-House: A film or TV presentation designed to be used internally by a corporation, government agency or special group. The film/tape is used for any or all of the following purposes: process explanation, orientation, information, motivation.

Inky-Dink: A popular term for a miniature incandescent lamp, usually 250 watt. Its main use is for highlighting part of a person or a prop, being a spotlight, not a FILL LIGHT. It is the smallest focusable LAMP.

Insert Shot: A DETAIL SHOT of the main scene, relevant to the action or mood. Used as a CUTAWAY SHOT to intensify and heighten the specific scene or to give necessary dramatic information: a key sentence in a letter, a date on a calendar, a newspaper headline, a face in a group photo, etc.

Instructional Film: A classroom or orientation film. Films used in the armed forces showing servicemen how to handle gear and arms are examples; as are films showing tellers how to "handle the window" or insurance agents the key points of a sale. An instructional film is designed to help teach or improve skills, obtain straightforward information or implant attitudes.

In Synch: 1. In technical use, meaning that sound and picture are synchronously joined. 2. Idiomatically, to be in accord. "Okay, then we agree; we're in synch."

Intercutting: The point and counterpoint of filmmaking, now being used more often in taping (production and postproduction) as well. Shots from other scenes and contexts inserted into the structure of an existing scene, for CONTRAST, suspense or comedic effects.

Interior: A scene that takes place indoors. The "interior" indication specifies "where." Abbreviated "int." in SCREENPLAYS.

Interlock System: Independent motors so controlled electrically that they all turn at precisely the same speed. The term is usually applied to any system by which picture and SOUND TRACKS may be projected synchronously, especially in dual-track MOVIOLAS and PROJECTORS.

Intermittent Movement: The basic mechanical principle of most motion picture cameras: to pull down and hold on each FRAME for the fraction of a second, thereby allowing for frame-by-frame exposure. In SOUND-SPEED cameras this rate is one frame every $1/_{24}$ second, or in nonfractional terms, 24 frames per second.

International Brotherhood of Electrical Workers: A UNION that began with stage electricians, then moved to the craft unions for stage and live TV, and finally for taped TV and motion pictures.

International Track: A separate track independent of the music and EFFECT tracks on which can be recorded NARRATION and/or DIALOGUE in whatever language is required by distribution commitments.

Internegative: Color NEGATIVE dupe struck from a color POSITIVE. Used for making RELEASE PRINTS, thereby avoiding touching the original.

Interpositive: A POSITIVE dupe used for making prints.

In the Can: 1. Exposed film, ready to go to the LAB. 2. Filming completed. "The picture's in the can!"

Iris Shutter: To be used in front of a SPOTLIGHT in order to go from a pinpoint beam to a large area, and all gradations in between. Its mechanism is quite similar to the iris shutter of a camera.

J

Jack Plug: A direct-connection device between audio components that plugs in at one or both ends.

Jam: A bunching up of the film going through the camera or projector so that it stops the mechanical drive and/or TAKE-UP movements.

Jellies, Color: Gelatin FILTERS placed in front of LAMPS. Also called GELS.

Joystick Zoom Control: Two-way switch (forward or reverse) attached to a cable connecting to a ZOOM-LENS drive motor. It can move the LENS for zoom-ins or zoom-outs, with either preset or variable speeds.

Juicer: An electrician, particularly one who handles the main power source.

Jump Cut: If a section is taken out of the middle of a shot, and the film respliced across the gap, a jump cut is said to result, since there is a jump in the shot's continuity. When the shot is motionless, this is a useful device for eliminating dead footage. Shots, however, are usually moving, and if there is movement, a visible jump will usually occur.

Junior: A focusable studio LAMP using a 2000-watt bulb and a FRESNEL LENS. The studio-lighting "basic" lamp.

Justified Camera Move: Organic camera movement, motivated by the action. A movement for a reason as opposed to random, distracting or unnecessary movement.

Juvenile: A young male role in a dramatic work. The age range is from the teens to mid-twenties. The masculine counterpart to the INGENUE.

K

K: 1. A call letter for radio and TV stations in the western half of the United States (as opposed to W for the eastern section, approximately west of the Mississippi): KSL (Salt Lake City); KOCE (PBS Station, Huntington Beach, California); KMPC (radio only, Los Angeles). There is some geographical overlapping: KQED in Pittsburgh, Pennsylvania. 2. An abbreviation and symbol for *kilowatt*. 3. An abbreviation and symbol for *Kelvin*, relative to the KELVIN SCALE.

Keep Takes: TAKES not recorded as out-takes (see OUTS), but as potential editing material out of which to make the completed film/take. Film takes that are to be printed are generally circled by the assistant cameraman and/or the SCRIPT CLERK. Also called *hold takes*.

Kelvin Scale: A scale for measuring and indicating COLOR TEMPERATURE. A Kelvin scale has the same gradation intervals as Centigrade.

Key Grip: Head of the GRIP crew.

Key Light: The main light used for the illumination of a particular subject within a scene. 1. *High-key lighting* is when the key light forms a very large proportion of the total illumination of the set, resulting in a low lighting CONTRAST and an effect of general brilliance in the scene. Still the recommended method for color shooting. 2. *Low-key lighting* is when the key light forms, in comparison with high-key lighting, a lower proportion of a smaller total illumination. The result is that many objects are allowed to fall into semidarkness or even total blackness, thus throwing others into correspondingly stronger relief. This more dramatic style of lighting, which has now won general acceptance for certain types of commercial films and is advancing even in color photography, makes greater demands on emulsion characteristics and on PROCESSING techniques than does high-key lighting.

Key Number: See EDGE NUMBER.

Keystoning: Distortion of image by its being projected at an angle other than perpendicular to the axis of the THROW, or caused by being filmed/taped at such an angle.

Kicker Light: A LAMP that puts light on the subject from behind and to the side. The light resulting from this.

Kill: To turn off some of the lights, as in "Kill the JUNIORS." Or, to turn off all the lights and stop the sound: "Okay! Kill everything!"

Kinescope: A film copy of a television program, filmed from the televised image.

Kinestasis: A neologism from the Greek, formed of "kine," indicating movement, and "stasis," denoting standing still. It refers to re-photographing a still photo, one FRAME at a time, for as many frames as necessary, usually 1 to 24 frames. A 48-frame shot (2 seconds) is one of long duration in kinestasic terms. When projected, the rapid cuts give a feeling of frenetic, staccato movement. Kinestasis is used for sequences of violence, fervid excitement, time compression, and general kaleidoscopic montages.

Klieg Light: Lights used originally in live theaters and eventually motion picture production. "Klieg light" in the 20's and 30's was synonymous with "movie light." It is a trade name.

L

Lab (Laboratory): In film usage, a company specializing in developing exposed motion picture stock, both for image and optical sound. The lab also makes MASTER POSITIVES, DUPE NEGATIVES and WORKPRINTS. Further, it runs off completed RELEASE PRINTS for the FILMMAKER and distributor. Many of the labs also have full postproduction videotaping facilities for tape-to-tape, film-to-tape or tape-to-film.

Lab Effects: Those OPTICAL EFFECTS that can be handled in LAB processing and printing: pushing light (see PUSH), printing for night effect, sepia-toning black-and-white stock, etc.

Lamp: General term for the electrical globes used in lighting the SET, no matter what size. Originally the word referred to the entire lighting unit, and still does in street, office or home lighting, but on a TV or film set, the word also refers to the globes.

Lamp Operator: A person in charge of a large LIGHTING unit that requires special attention.

Lap Dissolve: A lap dissolve is a long, overlapping DISSOLVE that has to be handled as special optical printing. It is sometimes differentiated from a dissolve, which is defined as merely the impression of one image fading away as another appears, done by using standard lab dissolves: 12, 24, 48 and 96 FRAMES.

Lapel Microphone: A small mike with a clip-on grip to attach to clothing, as near to the performer's mouth as possible.

Latent Image: The invisible image registered on a photographic emulsion, which becomes visible after development.

Latitude: The range of exposure of an emulsion. Latitude of exposure is normally greater than the latitude of an emulsion.

Laugh-Track: A SOUND TRACK of audience laughter used to augment actual studio laughter or added to a composite track that has no response on it at all. There are various kinds of laughter, from "tittering" to "uproarious," categorized and filed according to their texture by sound technicians.

Lavalier Microphone: A mike held to the performer by a cord around the neck.

Lay in: To spot and place shots or sound segments while assembling and structuring the flim.

Laying Tracks: Preparing and synching multiple sound tracks for the final MIXING sessions.

Lead: 1. The primary acting role in a SCREENPLAY or teleplay. From live theater terminology. There are usually at least two leads—the male and the female. 2. To pace the on-camera performer so that there is greater screen/camera-FRAME space in front of him in the cross-screen direction in which he is moving, than behind him.

Leader: Film consisting of a coated or uncoated stock used for THREADING in film-developing machines and sometimes for assembling WORKPRINT and re-recording SOUND TRACKS that contain only short segments of audio track. Different kinds of leader are designated by their color. (See also ACADEMY LEADER)

Lekolite: An ellipsoid spotlight with individual push-SHUTTERS for "shaping" the light. A live-theater standard and a "special" for TV and film.

Lens: A photographic lens consists of pieces of transparent substance called ELEMENTS. 1. A *long-focus lens* is a relative term describing lenses of greater FOCAL LENGTH than normal, and consequently giving greater than normal magnification. Incorrectly called TELEPHOTO LENS. 2. A *normal-focus lens* is 16mm (1 inch) or 35mm (2 inches). 3. A *short-focus lens* is a relative term describing lenses of shorter focal length than normal, consequently giving lower than normal magnification and a wider field of view. Also called WIDE-ANGLE LENS.

Lens Cap: Plastic or metal cover, using threaded or snap-on fitting, that attaches to the end of a LENS to protect it from scratches, dust, dampness, etc.

Lens Flare: A glint of light seen on the developed image, caused by sunlight or other bright illumination hitting the LENS.

Lens Hood, Lens Shade: A device to shield out unwanted light from striking the LENS. It is mounted on the lens barrel itself or directly in front of the camera.

Lens Markings: Calibration numbers and reference marks imprinted on a LENS to designate f-stop number, FOCUS and DEPTH OF FIELD.

Lens Mount: A device for attaching a LENS to a camera.

Lens Stop: An iris opening setting for a LENS, indicated by these standard f-stop numbers: 1.4, 2, 2.8, 4, 5, 6, 8, 11, 16 and 22. These numbers are derived from this formula: $f = \dfrac{\text{focal length}}{\text{diameter of opening}}$

Lens Support: A metal or plastic brace at the front end of a camera mount to support a long LENS.

Lens Tissue: Soft paper sheets with minimal lint, designed for cleaning glass LENSES.

Lens Turret: A LENS-mounting plate that can be rotated to accommodate two or more lenses. This allows quick movement from one lens to another, for varying FOCAL LENGTHS. Used often in early news-gathering on film and for documentary shooting. Now largely replaced by the ZOOM LENS.

Level: Volume of sound, usually registered by a needle indicator on a calibrated read-out meter.

Library Music/Effects: SCORING cues and SOUND EFFECTS that can be selected from "libraries" and transferred for postproduction laying in of tracks.

Light Board: A control board for distributing electrical current to lights for dimming, adjusting intensity or straightforward on and off.

Lighting: Photographic lighting is designated, like wind, by the direction from which it comes. 1. *Backlighting* is lighting from behind the SET or toward the camera. The actual light sources are shielded so as not to shine into the LENS. Backlighting increases lighting contrast up to the extreme condition of silhouette—no front light. 2. *Cross-lighting* is lighting intermediate in its direction and effect between front-lighting and backlighting. 3. *Front-lighting* is the main lighting of a SET from behind and beside the camera, that is, from in front of the set. The greater the proportion of front light to other kinds of light, the flatter the lighting, that is, the lighting contrast will be lower. 4. *Highlighting* is additional illumination applied to a small area. 5. *Top-lighting* is light from sources mounted above the subject and shining down onto it.

Light Level: Light intensity expressed in FOOT CANDLES, or candles per square foot.

Light Plot: Schematic indicating placement of lights on a SET or on LOCATION. Information on the plot gives LAMP names and wattage, and lamp positions.

Light-struck: Film that has been unintentionally exposed to light, causing EDGE FOGGING or full-frame FOGGING.

Light-struck Leader: Film deliberately exposed to the light, to be used as LEADER.

Light Trap: A darkroom entry with double doors, staggered black panels or other arrangements to let people in but keep light out.

Limbo Set: A SET suggesting open space, reaching to infinity. A CYCLORAMA is often used for a limbo set.

Limited Animation: ANIMATION wherein the main figures remain in place but segments are in motion, for example, the eyes or mouth.

Lines: 1. The principal FOREGROUND DIALOGUE, as opposed to the BACKGROUND burble of the crowd. 2. All the words in a SCRIPT to be spoken by the performers.

Lining up: The process by which a CAMERAMAN sets up his or her camera to cover the desired field of view. Also the adjustment of the MONITOR VIEWFINDER to correct for PARALLAX. Lining up is also called FRAMING.

Lip Synch: To match sound and picture to the actual movements of the lips, as opposed to matching FRAME numbers, edge-coded numbers (see EDGE NUMBER) or other referents. For the actor in LOOPING (see ADR), this means matching DIALOGUE to the actor on screen, dialogue of the actor himself/herself or another actor whose lines he/she is replacing, in the exact rhythm and basic style of the original lines.

Liquid-Gate Process: Machine that immerses film in a chemical solution that fills in scratches, thereby eliminating the refraction caused by the scratches and ensuring that they will not be projected onto the screen.

Listening Shot: A CUTAWAY SHOT of the person being spoken to listening to the actor delivering the dialogue. Used to intensify re-actions, to break up long speeches, or to cover a synch mistake by cutting to a listening shot and substituting a better audio take of the same dialogue.

Live Action: On-screen action of live performers, as opposed to ANIMATION.

Live Sound: Sound recorded on-the-spot during filming, as opposed to sound reproduced from prerecorded EFFECTS.

Location: Any place, other than the studio LOT, where units may be shooting a picture or making a VIDEOTAPE.

Location Manager: Production staff member in charge of scouting and/or logistics of a LOCATION shoot. Sometimes this is a line pro-ducer, UNIT MANAGER or production manager. (See also LOCATION SCOUT)

Location Scout: A person who goes ahead of the PRODUCTION UNIT, often weeks or months in advance, to shoot still pictures of potential LOCATION sites, check out contacts, accommodations, permits, and gather all charts, production sheets, names and statistics relating to the upcoming location shoots. (See also LOCATION MANAGER)

Logo: A visual symbol that immediately signifies a product or organization. Sometimes the logo is also the trademark.

Long Shot (LS): SHOT including the subject and his/or her surroundings. Or one of the subject at a great distance.

Loop: 1. A slack section of film designed to provide play when film is being fed from a continuously moving to an intermittently moving SPROCKET. 2. A continuous band of film that passes through a PROJECTOR or film reproducer in order to repeat a piece of ACTION or sound over and over again. Loops are used for instructional purposes, as guide tracks for DUBBING, and as convenient vehicles for continuous SOUND EFFECTS in re-recording.

Looping: Sound and/or voice augmentation or replacement of existing tracks. Voice looping often requires LIP SYNCH; at other times it can be to a specific CUE, as on OFF-SCREEN voice, but it still must fall on the exact FRAME. It is done by utilizing a continuous visual LOOP that is locked into a recording unit, and making a number of TAKES one after the other until the desired take(s), and often a protection take, are laid down. The SCENE-numbered takes are voice-slated and marked as to those preferred. (To voice-slate is to call off the number of the takes into a recording microphone.)

Loose Shot: One that has "breathing room": ample free space around the subject.

Lot: The grounds of a studio, including administration buildings, standing SETS, soundstages, and all structures, streets and encompassing fencing.

Low Angle: A camera position in which the camera is pointing upward. Low angles tend to make the on-camera performers look larger than life. The low angle intensifies the threat of a HEAVY or makes the protagonist more heroic in stature. Also called *low shot*.

Low-Key: Lighting that emphasizes the darker end of the lighting scale. (See also HIGH-KEY)

Low-Noise Lamps: LAMPS manufactured to emit minimal or no NOISE. This is so that the unwanted light-hum sound can be overcome and not picked up by the recording microphones.

M

Macrocinematography: Filming of small objects and details within photos or drawings by using a MACRO LENS, extension rings, diopters, etc.

Macro Lens: Detail LENS for extreme CLOSE-UP cinematography; tabletop filming. It can focus on an object extremely close to the camera.

Magazine, Film: Film containers forming an integral part of cameras (picture or sound) and projectors. Camera magazines are light-tight; the film enters and leaves them through light traps.

Magenta: Purplish color obtained by a mixture of red and blue light. A scene is balanced by reducing or increasing the magenta, or by letting it stay as is.

Magnetic Recorder: As opposed to optical recorder. A SOUND CAMERA that can play back the SOUND TRACK immediately upon RECORDING, without development.

Magnetic Sound: Sound recorded on magnetic tape, not on optical track or disk.

Magnetic Transfer: Going from one sound tape to another, usually from reel-to-reel ¼″ to 16mm or 35mm perforated magnetic SOUND STOCK. This stock is referred to familiarly as *mag stock*.

Main Title: 1. The graphic title that presents the name of the film. 2. Music that accompanies the graphic title.

Make up: To apply MAKEUP to the performer.

Makeup: The cosmetic supplies of the MAKEUP PERSON.

Makeup Person: One in charge of applying MAKEUP to the performers in preparation for their appearance in front of the camera. For makeup areas other than the hands and face, or for nude scenes, a special *body makeup person* is used. Also called *makeup artist*.

Manual Dimmer: Hand-operated light-dimmer board.

Marks: Visual guides to indicate where an actor is to be at a given point in the dialogue of a scene. On floors inside a studio, GAFFER'S TAPE or chalk is used for marking. In an open field an "X" might be drawn on the ground, or a rock put down as a stopping guide. In driving up to a gasoline pump within a scene, the actor's mark might be the center of the first pump. Anything preselected and agreed upon by director and actor as a stopping point is a mark.

Marquee: The signboard—usually cantilevered—in front of a theater. It has movable letters that spell out the names of the attractions and the stars and sometimes the admission price. Most contemporary marquees are built flush with the building area that houses the theater. This is especially true of motion-picture-theater clusters.

Married: 1. Picture and sound put together on one strip of film. 2. Burdened with, as in "Are we married to that piece of DIALOGUE or can we change it?"

Master Positive: A POSITIVE film with special photographic characteristics making it suitable for acting as a master from which a series of DUPE NEGATIVES can be printed with minimum loss of quality.

Master Scene: See MASTER SHOT.

Master Script: The final SHOOTING SCRIPT from which all others are duplicated.

Master Shot: The complete scene covering all dialogue and action in the widest and longest shot. Into this scene are added MEDIUM SHOTS, CLOSE-UPS, CUTAWAY SHOTS, etc. All of these shots are called *coverage.* Sometimes the problem of matching physical actions is handled by simultaneous multicamera filming/taping. But the master shot is the referent to which all else is edited, and to which all other action must be matched. Also called *master scene.*

Match Cut: Straight CUT from image to image in which the second image is structurally, compositionally or textually the same as the first.

Match Dissolve: A DISSOLVE that joins together filmically similar or symbolically analogous images.

Matching: 1. In LIVE-ACTION filming, the conformity of movement and camera direction. For example, a fight segment is always overlapped in its actions from the MASTER SCENE so that it can be cut on an appropriate matching FRAME. 2. In SCRIPT CONTINUITY, the visual conformity, from one day's shooting to the next, of wardrobe, hair, props, etc. A *mismatch* would be to see a man shaving, fully lathered (filmed on one day); he hears the doorbell ring, in a closer shot he turns (filmed on another day) and he is half-shaved.

Matching Stock: Noun: FILM STOCK of the same EMULSION NUMBER or lab number; or a stock that will effectively intercut (see INTER-CUTTING) with it. Verbal phrase: To either cut film or tape staged-action to match existing STOCK FOOTAGE. Or to shoot action and then find stock footage to match the action. The former is more practicable, preferable and frequent.

Matte: A light modulator that consists of an obstruction to the passage of light on its way to form a photographic image. Thus, mattes are not essentially different from *masks,* but the term "matte" is applied more often to the camera; "masks" to the color and optical printer.

Matte Bleed: An imperfect matted image, causing matte lines to be apparent.

Matte Box: A box mounted in front of a camera LENS and designed to hold camera MATTES used in SPECIAL EFFECTS photography. The matte box is usually combined with a sunshade and can also accommodate FILTERS.

Matte Finish: A softer, duller finish than glossy, giving a more diffused image.

Medium (Plural, Media): The particular communication form used in presenting the written material: radio, TV, CABLE, cassette, film, live performance, HOLOGRAPHY, AUDIO recording, or whatever medium or media are chosen. This could also include the *print media* (newspapers, magazines, periodicals), which are not the subject of this dictionary but are also referred to as media.

Medium Close-up (MCU): A shot framed (see FRAMING) to show part of the torso, the head and shoulders of the on-camera actor. See also CLOSE-UP.

Medium-long Shot (MLS): Between a MEDIUM SHOT and a LONG SHOT: a SHOT relevant to the establishment of those framings.

Medium Shot: A shot midway between a CLOSE SHOT and a LONG SHOT. These terms are therefore relative to what has been established as being close and long shots. In general parlance a medium shot is one that frames part of a person or object. In reference to a person it includes upper torso, the shoulders and head. The word "medium" can also be used to produce the terms MEDIUM CLOSE-UP and MEDIUM-LONG SHOT. "Medium-close" and "medium-long" in scripts are being replaced by the all-encompassing "medium shot" or by more descriptive and detailed instructions by the writer. Many scripts are now written, basically, in MASTER SCENES and leave the camera placement to the DIRECTOR.

Method Acting: Introspective and self-examining style of acting based on the work of Konstantin Stanislavsky, of the Moscow Art Theater. It utilizes techniques such as emotional recall, inner monologue, goal selection and motivation to concentrate the actor's energies in creating an inner reality. This entire procedure is referred to as *the Method*.

Metro–Goldwyn–Mayer (MGM): One of the major motion picture studios, located in Culver City, California. The Goldwyn part of the name was Sam Goldwyn, who left to set up his own studio and production company on what was formerly the United Artists lot. The Goldwyn Studios are now part of Warner Communications complex, and are called Warner's Hollywood. Louis B. Mayer stayed on to head MGM in Culver City.

Microphone Shadow: Cast by a microphone onto some object in the field of view of the camera. "Mike" shadows must be eliminated before shooting can begin, by altering the position of the microphone, the camera, the lights or the actors.

Miniature: A model used in films to appear its "normal" size. For example, a building is seen blowing up. Usually this is a scale model, for obvious reasons. Another example would be a square-rigged sailing ship burning and sinking. A miniature can be anything from a scale-model PROP to an entire SET or street.

Miscast: Chosen for a role but not having proper qualifications to fill it.

Mise-en-Scène: The total-action image, created by elements such as movement of performers, the setting itself, costumes, LIGHTING and PROPS. The full visual effect.

Mitchell: One of the major motion picture camera manufacturers. Most cameras in the major American studios and many of the international ones relied basically on the Mitchell as "the" camera, from the days of sound into the advent of the wide screen. It began to replaced in the late 50's and early 60's by the new, less-expensive lightweight and quiet-running cameras, or by self-blimped models from Europe, specifically the Arriflex, from Germany, and the Éclair, from France, and now, the CP-35mm.

Mix (Mixing): The process of combining a number of separate SOUND TRACKS into a single track.

Mixed Media: A blend into one program of any or all of these elements: LIVE ACTION, tape images, film, slides, graphics, special lighting and music, and SOUND EFFECTS. Disney's audioanimatronics shows often use film, live action, and audioanimatronic figures. The intermingling of STILL slides and LIVE ACTION is a common combination. Often used for trade shows, corporate-image extravaganzas and direct dramatized sales pitches.

Mixer: The senior member of a sound-recording crew, who is in charge of the balance and control of the DIALOGUE, music, or SOUND EFFECTS to be recorded.

Mixing Board: Another name for the console used in a mixing session. It allocates channels to separate audio tracks and blends them into a mixed-track.

Modeling Lights: KEY LIGHTS and FILL LIGHTS, for example. LIGHTING units that create BACKLIGHTING, HIGHLIGHTS, shadows on actors and the setting. Distinguished from BACKGROUND or SET lights.

Module: An interlinking component in an electronic system.

Monitor: Noun: The screen on which televised images can be evaluated either in the studio or in the control room. In a TV-control situation each camera has its own monitor screen with a master screen that shows which camera has been chosen for a given segment of coverage. Verb: To oversee production images or sound.

Monologue: Extended speech for a single person. A monologue can be part of a scene, for example, an instructor briefing a class. Or it can be isolated, as when Hamlet either walks away from the others in the scene to deliver his monologue or when he is discovered alone and gives the speech. Then too, the monologue in film or on tape can be delivered in SYNCH SOUND or by the off-screen voice of the actor being heard as if it were his or her thoughts unraveling.

Montage: As used in commercial studios, the term means a type of cutting using numerous CUTS, DISSOLVES and superimpositions rapidly following one another to produce a total visual effect.

Mood Music: Synonym for *background music*, particularly indicating music that arouses appropriate emotional responses in the audience, relevant to a given scene.

MOS: Slate indication noting that a particular SHOT is without sound. The legend is that a German director called out, "This shot is mitout sound," and the sound man answered, "Mark it MOS—Mit Out Sound." The truth is that it is an early film abbreviation for *minus optical sound*.

Motion Picture Association of America: A group for promoting the international dissemination of American films and upgrading the imported product. One of its functions is the assigning of audience ratings: G for general audience, PG for parental guidance, R for restricted and X for adults only.

Motion Picture Projector: A machine that throws film-images onto a screen. Projectors in motion picture theaters are usually 35mm or wide-screen format 65/70mm, sometimes augmented by a 16mm projector; such projecters are all sound-equipped. For home movies and nonprofessional filming, 8mm, Super-8 and SUPER-16 are the most common film-widths; such projectors come in both silent and sound models.

Movie: Another name for *motion picture*.

Moviola: The trade name of a particular kind of portable motor-driven film-viewing machine used in cutting (see CUT, CUTTER). The name is often applied generically to any such machine.

Multi-image: Two or more simultaneous separate pictures on the film or TV screen. This is done by fractionating the screen into discrete images, as in *split-screen*, or by overlapping the images as in a DISSOLVE or superimposition. Fast-cut sequential images, as in KINESTASIS, are sometimes described as multi-image.

Multimedia: See MIXED MEDIA.

Musical Comedy: A form often filmed or televised. Developed from the English musical stage and the Spanish zarzuela. Originally a play punctuated by musical numbers, later developments in America and England have resulted in many of the newer works being fully musical, through-composed musical-dramatic works, deriving more from opera in structure. Then too there has been a tendency for book and lyrics to be more substantive, so that the "comedy" part of a musical comedy is often seriocomic or even tragic. This has resulted in a more frequent use of the simplified expression *musical*.

Musical Contractor: Person responsible for hiring the musical performers or orchestra members or for subcontracting a complete musical-performing unit.

Musical Director: Person in charge of seeing that music is composed and/or selected for the film/tape and is orchestrated and copied. Also supervises the actual SCORING sessions, and in some cases conducts them. The composer sometimes also serves as musical director.

Music Library: An index or catalogue of the music and SOUND TRACKS of which a studio may wish to make repeated use. Also, the music sound tracks themselves.

N

Nagra: Standard professional portable tape recorder, using $1/4''$ reel-to-reel magnetic tape.

Narration: OFF-SCREEN commentary spoken by a "name" NARRA-TOR, that is, a well-known personality in the media (see MEDIUM) or another field, or by an anonymous "voice-of-God" narrator who gives the words their tone of authority. Most INFORMATIONAL FILMS utilize an anonymous narrator. In a dramatic film or tape, the narrator may be one of the characters in the story.

Narration Script: A SCRIPT that is double- or triple-spaced, containing primarily narration text, with only absolutely necessary SCENE indications. Used for recording the NARRATOR's voice-over tracks.

Narrator: The voice-over commentator who relates the story or explains points of information.

Narrow-Gauge Film: Any strip of film narrower than the standard 35mm.

National Broadcasting Company (NBC): Along with ABC and CBS, one of the three major television networks.

Naturalism: A style of realism showing characters floating on the tide of social events over which they have minimal or no control. Human values are implied rather than didactically stated.

Nature Film: A motion picture about the natural environment—plants, animals, geographical features.

Negative: The term is used to designate any of the following: 1. RAW STOCK specifically designed for a negative image. 2. The NEGATIVE IMAGE. 3. Negative raw stock that has been exposed but not PROCESSED. 4. Processed film bearing a negative image. Related terms are: *original picture negative*: the original picture negative film that is exposed in the camera and subsequently processed, *original sound negative*: the original sound negative exposed in a film recorder, and *picture negative*: any negative film which, after exposure to a subject or positive image and subsequent processing, produces a negative picture image on the film.

Negative Cost: The total cost of a film production in all its aspects prior to RELEASE. Differentiated from distribution, subdistribution and exhibition costs.

Negative Cutting: The cutting of the original NEGATIVE of a film to match the edited POSITIVE, SHOT-by-shot and FRAME-by-frame. The large FOOTAGE to be catalogued, the necessity for exact correspondence of frame with frame, and the irreplaceability of the negative, impose very exacting conditions on negative CUTTERS. Also called *negative matching*.

Negative Filter: An optical FILTER that attenuates those parts of the spectrum which are predominant constituents of daylight: the blue from the sky and the green reflected from trees and grass. Consequently, NIGHT FILTERS are red and are used to produce night effects by day, or black and white film. They require a large FILTER FACTOR to compensate for the amount of light they absorb. Night filters are a type of EFFECTS filter.

Negative Image: A photographic image in which the values of light and shade of the original photographed subject are represented in inverse order.

Negative Numbers: Same as EDGE NUMBERS, but more commonly used by manufacturers of RAW STOCK.

Negative Perforation 35mm: The perforation used for NEGATIVE and some special-purpose 35mm film.

Negative-Positive Process: Generic term for the normal process of 35mm black and white image reproduction whereby positive images are printed from NEGATIVES and vice versa. In other words, any film generates unlike, whereas in the reversal process it generates likes.

Neorealism: Emerged in Italy after World War II with films such as Rossellini's *Open City* and De Sica's *Shoeshine* and *The Bicycle Thief*. These films, and others in their genre, were filmed almost entirely on location with few professional actors, utilizing the people in the community as actors instead, and strongly accenting the harsh realism of existence.

Neutral Density: A group of gray FILTERS with graded densities, used to minimize CONTRAST and cut down EXPOSURE.

New Wave: Films by young French directors that emerged in the late 50's and early 60's. The films used the new professional and lightweight sound and camera and real-life settings, avoided soundstages, and attempted a more psychological approach to characters than emphasis on plot, the "realism" coming from the true-life locales. Also called *nouvelle vague*.

NG Takes: Unusable shots, made so by error from equipment, crew or cast. NG is the abbreviation for "no good." The term is also used for shot records, sound reports, camera reports, and production and SCRIPT CLERKS' notes: "NG sound," "NG action," etc.

Night Filter: One that cuts down EXPOSURE or changes the overall color-tint of a daylight shot so that a nighttime effect is created.

Noise: Any extraneous sound tending to interfere with the proper and easy perception of desired sounds to be recorded. Unwanted noise can be internal to the systems, or external, such as an air conditioner or outside traffic.

Noiseless Camera: A camera that has internal NOISE-traps; self-blimped.

Nonhero: Leading character in a literary or dramatic work who is not noble, uses wiles to seek his or her ends, and often does not attain them. Alfie, in the film by that name, is an example, as is Archie

Rice in *The Entertainer*. In literature the first "modern" nonhero was probably Fielding's Jonathan Wild. Also called *antihero*.

Nontheatrical: A term applied to the showing of films outside commercial movie theaters.

Nudie: A motion picture film exploiting the nude form, female and male, in a usually lightly plotted "story." Nudies came in during the 50's as precursors of the general-admission porno films.

Numbering Machines: A machine for printing EDGE NUMBERS at regular intervals on RAW STOCK. The term is sometimes used when CODING MACHINE is meant.

Nuts-and-Bolts Film: A straightforward film describing processes or skills, or implanting information. A HOW-TO FILM is an example of a nuts-and-bolts film.

O

Oater: Western film. A HORSE OPERA.

Objective Camera: The viewpoint of a spectator looking at a scene, as opposed to SUBJECTIVE CAMERA.

Obligatory Scene: 1. The original meaning, still in use academically, is that of an action that is a logical outcome of the scenes which precede it. 2. In the media (see MEDIUM) markets the term refers to a scene that must be included in order to secure audiences: the nude scene, the superviolent scene, the graphic love scene. In this sense it is a synonymic phrase for *gratuitous scene*, which implies one called for not by dramatic logic but by eager distributors.

Off-Camera: Outside the viewing range of the scene being filmed/taped. Just outside the perimeter of the action.

Off-Line: Preparing tapes by evaluating and/or editing them for final ON-LINE mix.

Off-Mike: Outside the live-range pattern of a microphone.

Off-Screen (OS): Not in the FRAME but immediately at hand. A single REVERSE in a TWO-SHOT, for example, means that the person not on-camera is off-screen. The voice of the actor who is not seen but is nearby is referred to as being off-screen. Not to be confused with *voice-over (VO)*, which means that the voice of an anonymous narrator, or the voice of one not physically in or at the scene, is speaking.

OK Takes: As opposed to NG TAKES. These are good takes from which the editor and director will make their final choices in putting together the completed film.

Omnimax System: A special lens system to be mounted and utilized with the IMAX camera.

On Call: A CREW or CAST member officially notified and waiting for time and place to be given for filming/taping.

One-Light Print: A noncorrected print using one printing light at a preset level for all shots.

Ones: In ANIMATION, the one-to-one EXPOSURE of one FRAME per one drawing: "We're shooting it in ones."

One-Shot: A shot of a single person. Also called a *single*. TWO-SHOT means two people; *three-shot*, three, and so on. Over four or five is generally described as a *group shot*.

On Hold: Having been given a working STANDBY call, to be fully paid for the day but not have to report to the SET or LOCATION. When the CAST or CREW member is on hold, he or she must be immediately accessible by phone, as they must be available in case they are called to the production locale on short notice.

On-Line: 1. All pre-edited tapes tied in to the tape-mastering units for the full mix. (See also MIX) 2. State of doing the final tape edit, utilizing audio/video components prepared in the OFF-LINE sessions.

On Spec (Speculation): Producing a film with no negative pickup or distribution deal; one designed to make its returns on sales and rentals.

Onstage: Physically present on the performing stage, as opposed to OFFSTAGE. This term is also used by directors to refer to the lighted performing area of a TV or film set.

Opaque Leader: Optically opaque filmstrips of the same size as the film being edited. Used to space FRAME-to-frame in A-ROLL and B-ROLL cutting.

Open-End Films: Films that state in dramatic and/or narrative style a given problem or situation, deliberately leaving it unresolved in order to stimulate group discussion.

Optical Dupe: A DUPE NEGATIVE printed in an optical printer, usually containing OPTICAL EFFECTS.

Optical Effects: Modifications of the photographic image as filmed in a motion picture camera of normal type, produced in an optical printer.

Optical House: A business that specializes in customized optical printing and/or SPECIAL EFFECTS.

Optical-Sound Recorder: Equipment incorporating means for producing a modulated light beam and for moving a light-sensitive medium relative to the beam for recording signals derived from sound signals.

Option: Negotiated access to fully purchase a film or TV property, usually secured by payment of an *option fee*. The contract specifies a given date by which the film or TV property must be in production, or the option expires and the property reverts to the author; unless of course there is a full buyout upfront.

Order of Appearance: A listing in the screen CREDITS of the performers as they are seen on-screen in chronological order. This makes it easier for the performers to be identified, and often solves problems of BILLING. Another way of listing is by alphabetical order.

Original: A generic film term applied either to a film scene or to the first recording of that scene. Since film processes are marked by sequential modification (how many generations away the print is from the original), the concept of an original is of great importance in setting up standards of comparison.

Original Screenplay: A SCRIPT that is created by a writer from his or her concept and story and not adapted from a book, play or other literary work. (See also SCREENPLAY).

Orthochromatic: Applied to emulsions, orthochromatic means a type sensitive to blue and green but not to red. Applied to photographic reproductions, it means the true REPRODUCTION of colors in black and white.

OS: The abbreviation for OFF-SCREEN.

Oscar: The nickname—which has become the fully accepted name—of the statuette awarded for various categories at the annual ACADEMY AWARDS, presented by the ACADEMY OF MOTION PICTURE ARTS AND SCIENCES.

Outline: An early treatment of the idea of a film. A rough sketch of the filmmaker's intended approach to his or her subject.

Out of Synch: When the picture doesn't match the sound. That is, if the person is seen talking, but for a moment or two no sound is heard; or if you hear dialogue before the lips begin to move; or if you see a dish hit the floor and, after a delayed beat, hear the sound. Or the reverse of all of the above. (See also SYNCHRONISM)

Outs: Rejected takes of the same basic shots, not used in the completed version of the film. Also called *out-takes*.

Overcrank: Running the camera more rapidly than standard speed. This faster-than-normal operation results in a slowing down of the motion on the screen.

Overhead Shot: From directly above, looking down on the action.

Overlap: 1. In DIALOGUE cutting, the extension of a dialogue SOUND TRACK over a shot to which it does not belong. A REACTION SHOT of the person being addressed on the OVERLAPPING-SOUND track. 2. In acting, to keep the dialogue moving, with one line starting before the lead-in line is completed. Talking at the same time: "That was an overlap." "Be sure to overlap the incoming lines of dialogue." Sometimes in recording "wild" lines it is important to do them singly with space in between for the editor to separate them effectively. In this case, the RECORDIST will tell the actors doing their dialogue "wild": "Don't overlap." This means to leave a beat or two between lines. (See also "WILD" RECORDING)

Overlapping Action: Picking up the action of the next sequential shot with part of the concluding action of the preceding shot, then "matching" them in the process of editing.

Overlapping Sound: Sound from the preceding shot carried forward into the following shot. Or sound from the shot coming up that is heard at the end of the preceding shot. This latter use is also called *foreshadowing sound*.

Overload: 1. Pulling more current than the immediate electrical system can supply, often causing a fuse or circuit-breaker blowout. 2. Recorded at too high a level, resulting in sound distortion, NOISE or feedback.

Over-the-Shoulder (OTS): A shot from behind and to the side of the FOREGROUND actor, including part of the head and shoulder. The camera is pointing in the direction in which the actor is looking.

P

Package: A total presentation of the basic elements needed to do a film or TV series or special. The professional package minimally consists of a SCRIPT, a BUDGET, a SHOOTING SCHEDULE and often commitments by a STAR or stars and a DIRECTOR. It can also be enhanced by indicating agreed-upon deferments (payments delayed until after release of the film at various stages of repayment) from LAB, performers or director, and having part of the funding already raised or agreed upon when the corrected ANSWER PRINT or completed tape is delivered to the distributors.

Packet Switch: Message-transmission term indicating a complete message that is assembled into one or more *packets* that can be transmitted through the network, then reassembled at the receiving destination into the original message.

Page: 1. As a means of time measurements. The query "How many pages did you shoot today?" is one that has been relevant from the days of silent films when the longer and fully scripted scenarios began to make their appearance, replacing the OUTLINE or gag setup. A SCREENPLAY page—in running time—averages about 50 seconds to a minute. Of course, if the $1/_8$ of a page reads: "The two armies engage," the page may run a little longer in time. But even with these variations, the screenplay pages usually total up at the end of the shooting to approximately a minute a page. It is a working practice in films, and also in film/tape dramatic feature-length specials, to schedule a given number of pages on a specified shooting. "We're a page and a half behind," is a common complaint of PRODUCERS and PRODUCTION MANAGERS. 2. A large TV station's usher for audience programs. Also serves as a guide who takes groups on tours of the facilities.

Paid Spot: A commercial-announcement segment of time paid for by a sponsor instead of having the time provided for by the station as in a PSA (public service announcement). The paid spot also refers to the taped or filmed COMMERCIAL itself.

Painter Light: Meticulously calibrated and regulated source of illumination in a lab printer.

Pan: 1. Movement of the camera in a horizontal plane. Sometimes used generally to describe movements of the camera in any plane. "That was a smooth pan." "Pan to your left." 2. To negatively criticize a film, radio or TV production. Term popularized by *Daily Variety*.

Pan-and-Tilt Head: Camera mount allowing camera rotation around both a vertical and horizontal axis.

Panchromatic: A type of light-sensitive emulsion RECORDING in black and white that is almost equally responsive to all colors of the visible spectrum. Other common types of emulsion are ORTHOCHROMATIC and COLORBLIND.

Panchromatic Film: Black and white film sensitive to all colors, providing a full range of gray tones.

Pan Focus: A DEPTH-OF-FIELD setting deep and wide enough to allow everything in the ACTION field to remain in FOCUS.

Pantomime: The silent portrayal of a dramatic incident or mood without recourse to speech. Pantomime is used often in COMMERCIALS, utilizing realistic, stylized or even classic white-faced mime. The silent films relied entirely on mime, mimetic action, dance or acrobatics.

Paper-to-Paper: Film marked off by paper tape or paper insert tags, indicating start-here/stop-here. Used in rolling down to a section of ORIGINAL film to be printed in a lab, or to a film scene to be projected or transferred to VIDEOTAPE.

Parabolic Reflector: A large concave dish-shaped receptor to pull in maximum signals and pinpoint-focus them into an attached microphone. Used for conventions, sporting events, parades and other occasions where great areas or distant spots must be covered.

Parallax: The difference between the image seen by the eye through the VIEWFINDER and that seen by the camera LENS. In FRAMING a picture, this has to be taken into consideration, since areas may be cut off due to this error. Parallax is eliminated in cameras with reflex viewing systems, since the eye sees through this lens itself.

Parallax Error: Faultily framed image caused by not correcting the compositional shift from the parallax-finder. Not compensating for parallactic distortion of apparent angle.

Parallel: A fixed platform that can be set up in the studio or on LOCATION to raise the camera and crew above the ground for HIGH SHOTS. Also can be used for holding lights.

Paramount: One of the remaining major studios still operating in HOLLYWOOD. WARNER BROTHERS is in Burbank and in the former Goldwyn Studios facility in central Hollywood. But MGM is in Culver City, COLUMBIA PICTURES is centered at the Burbank Studios, and Twentieth Century–Fox is in West Los Angeles. The old RKO (then DESILU) studios have been joined to the Paramount complex.

Patch: A film overlay, cemented to two abutting pieces of film to join them together. The purpose: to repair a damaged NEGATIVE without losing FRAMES.

Pathos: Emotional texture in a work of art that evokes a feeling of sympathy in the audience.

PBS: The abbreviation for PUBLIC BROADCASTING SYSTEM.

Pencil Test: A procedure using pencil drawings to check out an ANIMATION move for speed and smoothness before going to the next step, painting the cels.

Persistence of Vision: A phenomenon that causes an image on the retina to be mentally retained for a short period, so that if a second similar image takes its place within a period of about $1/16$ of a second, no visible discontinuity will be noticed. This is the visual basis for the motion picture.

Personal Direction: See GENERAL DIRECTION.

Photoplay: (Obsolescent) Another name for SCREENPLAY, SCRIPT (film), or *scenario*.

Picture Car: Any car, truck or van that appears in front of the camera as an "actor," as opposed to, for example, a CAMERA CAR. (See also HONEY WAGON)

Picture Image: The visual likeness of an object recorded photographically on the film; or on tape, HOLOGRAM or VIDEODISK.

Pincushion Distortion: A LENS characterized by concave curvature of the lines of a rectangular grid image, caused by magnification that is less at the center than at the edges of the field.

Pipe: An actual plumber's pipe or specially made rigging-pipe that can be hung from a grid or other overhead device on which lights can be mounted.

Pix: Popular trade-journalese for "pictures." Popularized by *Daily Variety* and *Billboard*.

PL: Phone line for headphone-microphone set going from taping area to control room or taping vehicle, for establishing communications between the taping area and the control unit.

Platen: The flat-glass transparent plate that holds down ANIMATION material to be filmed on an ANIMATION STAND.

Play: A dramatic work for one or more ACTORS, in one or more acts. A stage term designating a piece designed originally for live theater, which may later be adapted for film or television, or the concept purchased as the basis for a series.

Playback: 1. A term used to denote immediate REPRODUCTION of a RECORDING. 2. A method of filming singing and other types of musical action in which the music is recorded first (called PRERECORDING) and afterward played back through loudspeakers on the soundstage, thus enabling the singers or dancers to perform to the music while being filmed with an unsilenced camera under imperfect acoustical conditions. This action is afterward synchronized with the original recording made under substantially perfect acoustic conditions.

Player: Term for ACTOR/performer often used in contracts as a comprehensive name for any on-camera person (or radio or live-theater person), as opposed to PRODUCER.

Plot: The skeletal story of a dramatic work that gives it its inherent structure. To be differentiated from CHARACTERIZATION, THEME, SUBTEXT.

Point of View (POV): A subjective viewpoint, looking at the scene of action with the camera serving as the "eyes" of one of the characters, and the setting and movement as seen from that viewpoint.

Portable Dressing Room: Dressing room on small wheels that can be rolled from one shooting stage to another to augment permanent dressing room space or work closer to the SET. A dressing room that can be trucked or hauled as a trailer, or a mobile home that can be used on LOCATION. (See also HONEY WAGON)

Positive (Print): The term *positive* or *print* is used to designate any of the following: 1. The RAW STOCK specifically designed for positive image. 2. The positive image. 3. Positive RAW STOCK that has been exposed but not processed. 4. Processed film bearing a positive image.

Postsynchronization: The addition of speech or SOUND EFFECTS to synchronize with picture images that already have been shot. (See also DUBBING)

Practical: An operational prop that functions during the filmed/taped scene. For example, a TV that is playing in the living-room set, a table lamp that can be turned on, a one-armed bandit that works.

Practical Set: A real LOCATION, not a studio SET. An actual drugstore might be used instead of constructing a "drugstore set," for example. As location sound improves and studio construction-costs rise, there is a great financial incentive to shoot more and more scenes on practical sets.

Premiere: Official opening of a theatrical film in a specially chosen theater, or the screening of the first segment of a new TV series.

Prerecording: Recording of music or other sound prior to the shooting of the picture to accompany it, and in predetermined SYNCHRONISM.

Presence: The sound AMBIENCE of a specific locale, recorded by itself before and/or after a sound take. Used to fill in sound DROPOUTS or to use as general BACKGROUND to mix with DIALOGUE replacement tracks. (See also ROOM TONE)

Presence Loop: A sound LOOP that runs continuously through a scene during a sound mix to fill in dead spots or DROP-OUTS. It is either a "wild" sound presence recording (see "WILD" RECORDING) in the same spot where the scene was filmed or a simulation of the sound of that locale.

Pressure Plate: In a camera, projector or optical printer, a plate that presses on the back of the film in order to keep the emulsion surface even with the FOCAL PLANE of the LENS.

Primary Colors: Blue, green and red. The various mixtures of the colors of light, from which all other colors can be produced.

Process: To develop and/or print ORIGINAL film.

Processing: The group of operations comprising the developing, fixing, hardening, washing and drying of black and white film, and with any other processes required to produce a NEGATIVE or POSITIVE with a satisfactory visible image from a strip of film carrying a corresponding latent image.

Process Projection: A composite studio technique whereby the ACTORS, SETS and PROPS in front of the camera are combined with a BACKGROUND that consists of a translucent screen on which a picture is projected from behind. Also called *back projection, background projection, transparency process,* and, more recently, FRONT PROJECTION.

Producer: The person who carries ultimate responsibility for the original shaping and final outcome of a film.

Product Bonus: An extra print or tape given as a bonus when a school system or corporation buys a large number of prints or tapes.

Production: The general term used to describe the processes involved in making all the original materials that are the basis for the finished motion picture.

Production Manager: The person who supervises the daily production of a film, working directly with the ASSISTANT DIRECTOR, PRODUCER, and DIRECTOR. He or she relays orders from the director and producer to the AD, as well as overseeing the signing of contracts, catering, daily accountancy, scouting of locations, and permit arrangements for all nonstudio shoots. His role is similar to and overlaps the responsibility of the assistant director.

Production Notes: Notes and reports made during filming/taping of all aspects of PRODUCTION: camera and sound reports, PRODUCTION MANAGER's reports, SCRIPT CLERK's notes, etc. Used during production and in postproduction. Also called *production report*.

Production Unit: A self-contained group consisting of DIRECTOR, camera crew, sound crew, ELECTRICIANS, etc., which works on a soundstage or on LOCATION to shoot an assigned picture or section of a picture.

Professional: A performer or crew member paid for his or her services. More broadly, an attitude: "Why don't you approach it in a more professional way?"

Projection Speed: Rate at which film is projected: 18 FPS for silent film, 24 FPS for sound film.

Projector: A device by which films are viewed by throwing an image on a large *screen*. Classified as *sound* or *silent*.

Props (Properties): The term has the same meaning in film production as in theater production: items to be photographed in a SCENE, ranging from furniture to cigarette lighters.

Public Broadcasting System (PBS): A loose affiliation of stations that handles special educational, documentary, in-depth news and other programs not generally carried by the major TV networks—ABC, CBS and NBC. These programs tend to be more substantive than standard major network fare. PBS consists of more than 300 stations that exchange programming with one another.

Public Service Announcement (PSA): An announcement in a time spot reserved for a COMMERCIAL. The announcement is presented without a time fee by the radio/TV station as a public service. PSAs are for nonprofit and charitable organizations such as United Way, American Red Cross, and Boy Scouts of America.

Pull: A term used by the electrical crew to indicate how much power will be drawn off and used by a particular LAMP or lamps. "What does it pull?" "It's pulling ten amps!"

Pull Back: To move the camera away from the point of action. Also given as a direction even when using a ZOOM LENS, as in "Okay, get ready to pull back," meaning *zoom out.*

Punch: 1. Hand punch for marking a hole in film LEADER to indicate starting point for either the editor, MIXER or LAB. 2. A mechanical device for making holes on the edge of an ANIMATION or title card to match the pegs on an ANIMATION STAND or easel.

Purchasing Consortium: Groups that band together in order to get more favorable rates on volume purchasing of film prints or VIDEO-TAPES.

Push: To give instructions to the LAB to allow the film to stay in the developer for the length of time necessary to expose it one, two or however many stops are necessary and possible. To add this additional exposure-time is known as "pushing" the film.

Push-over Wipe: A wipe in which the first image moves horizontally across the screen, as if propelled by the second image, which immediately follows it, much as in a lantern-slide projector when slides are being changed.

Q

Q-TV: Trade name for a TV or film cueing system in which the reflected image of DIALOGUE is seen on a beveled sheet of plate glass directly in front of the camera, but because of the angle is not seen by the camera lens.

Quarter-Inch Tape: Standard width of reel-to-reel magnetic recording tape.

Quartz Light: Informal term for the tungsten-HALOGEN group of LAMPS. These longer-lasting globes are becoming the basic lights for production, augmented by other lamps such as arcs and incandescents.

Quickie: A film or tape put together, filmed and released on a short schedule in order to save time and money and/or to make a release deadline. As a rule, synonymous with *low-budget*. Often carries with it a derogatory connotation as to the quality of the film.

Quiet: A command called out directly or amplified over a bullhorn or loudspeaker. It precedes the command "ROLL," the response "SPEED," and the command "ACTION." It is generally given by the ASSISTANT DIRECTOR, who then signals to the DIRECTOR when the appropriate state of working silence has been achieved.

Quip: A witty or sarcastic fast retort, a rehearsed (or sometimes real) AD-LIB, used especially in COMEDY routines or to provide comedic flavor in an interview program or game show.

R

Rack Focus: A lens-shift to bring an out-of-focus background image into the foreground, thereby throwing the foreground image out of focus. Or vice versa.

Radio: (Verb) Used as a direction or command in walkie-talkie or two-way radio communication in filming where the DIRECTOR and camera are separated. "Radio us just before you're starting to turn in your helicopter" is a typical direction from a ground-based director to a CAMERAMAN making an aerial shot.

Radio Corporation of America (RCA): A parent corporation that holds patents on radio and TV components, designs, trademarks, etc. It put together the NATIONAL BROADCASTING COMPANY and Victor Records as major adjuncts of its corporate structure.

Radio Mike: Microphone not connected by wire but operating on a matching radio frequency with the receiving unit. A microphone and mini-transmitter are clipped and/or taped to the actor. DIALOGUE is received by the receiving unit, which feeds directly into the recorder or to a premix and/or amplifying unit.

Ramp: Improvised slanted incline, with or without tracks, on which to move a DOLLY smoothly alongside actors as they move up or down stairways or over rough terrain.

Rate Sheet: A photocopied or printed page or brochure listing services and costs. Given out by production-service companies such as LABS, sound-recording studios, equipment-rental houses, sound-stage facilities and graphics shops.

Raw Stock: Film that has not been exposed (see EXPOSURE) or processed (see PROCESSING).

Reaction Shot: A SHOT in which an ACTOR reacts to what has happened or what has been said in a specific point of a SCENE. Generally, this is a CUTAWAY SHOT.

Reader (Sound Reader): Editing unit with manual or motor-driven mechanism to roll magnetic and/or optical sound through the machine. The sound is audited on a self-contained loudspeaker in the reader, or by jack-plugging into it with earphones.

Reconditioning: Treatment of NEGATIVES and prints with the object of removing oil, scratches and abrasions from their surface.

Recording: The act of producing a copy of a visible and audible event in the external world.

Recording, Live: A RECORDING of an original sound, as distinguished from RE-RECORDING. Also called an original recording.

Recording System: A combination of microphones, mixer, amplifiers and a film recorder, which is often used for recording sound with a picture.

Recordist: The actual operator of the sound camera.

Reduction Printing: Printing down from a larger-gauge film to a smaller, in order to get a COMPOSITE PRINT in the narrower gauge.

Reel: 1. A metal or plastic spool carrying a small positioning notch and spoked FLANGES or side pieces on which the film is wound. According to prevailing professional practices, POSITIVE film is at all times kept wound on reels after it has left the laboratory. 2. The metallic or plastic circular holder for feeding out and taking up film in filming, editing or projection. 3. Used as a term to describe the approximate length of a film: "A 1000-foot reel of 35mm, running about ten minutes." A *two-reeler* is about twenty minutes long. Most contemporary features (see FEATURE LENGTH) run between nine to twelve reels, although new projection techniques with FLANGE or open-reel feed-out allow entire features to be put onto one extra large reel, or *film roll*.

Reel-to-Reel: A transfer term in sound recording, generally meaning making a copy from one format to the same format, for example, going from $1/4''$ sound recording to tape to the same $1/4''$ from the copy. Or going from $3/4''$ VIDEOTAPE to a $3/4''$ copy.

Reflector: A reflecting surface, frequently silver in color, used to reflect light to a point where it is needed. For exteriors, reflectors are often used to direct sunlight onto the actors or some other part of the scene. For interior lighting, they are used to bounce light from source to action area. 1. A *hand reflector* is a lightweight reflector, small enough to be worked manually. 2. A *hard reflector* is a highly polished silver or aluminum-foil surface giving a mirrorlike reflection. 3. A *soft reflector* is one that is coated with silver or gold. It is softer in color than a hard reflector, and is pebbled to diffuse the reflected light. 4. A *reflector stand* is a special holder, usually metal, for the reflector. It comes in two basic sections: the YOKE, which holds the reflector, and the *stand*, which supports the yoke.

Registering: The reaction of an on-camera performer to the dialogue, action or general situation of the scene. A common directorial complaint to an actor is: "You're listening but nothing's registering."

Registration: Proper alignment of film in a rigid position. In ANIMATION, the precision placement of layers of cels.

Release: A generic term used to designate a completed film used for general distribution or exhibition.

Release Negative: A complete NEGATIVE prepared specifically for printing RELEASE PRINTS.

Release Print: A COMPOSITE PRINT made for general distribution. This occurs after the final trial composite or SAMPLE PRINT has been approved.

Remake: Noun: A full new production and release of a film made in earlier years. Examples: *A Star is Born, Stagecoach, Beau Geste, King Kong.* Verb: "We're going to remake D. W. Griffith's *Intolerance.*"

Rembrandt Lighting: Overall "painting with light," characterized by rim-lighting, contrasting light-and-dark areas, and a general sense of what directors refer to as "mood" and PRODUCTION MANAGERS as "expensive." Rembrandt lighting also can be used to delineate the nature of the characters in the scene.

Remote: A radio or TV broadcast from a field unit away from the home studio. Conventions, sporting events, on-the-spot news are all examples of remotes.

Replay: The immediate running of a tape take to check it for use or exclusion in the final edited edition by viewing it on a playback monitor. Also called a *playback*.

Reports: These are written in production ledgers or on a special pad daily. Sound and camera reports, for example, which indicate acceptable and nonacceptable TAKES and additional relevant material, are made out on special long, rectangular pads with multiple carbons to annotate each take. *Production reports* are prepared by line producers and unit managers. They contain the work hours for each member of the cast and crew, the amount of film stock shot, costs of the shooting day, number of PAGES filmed, balance of pages yet to shoot, location and scouting data—in brief, everything essential to the logistics of a shoot. The SCRIPT CLERK's notes can also be classified under the heading of production reports.

Reproduction: The reproduction of the world of colors in the convention of black and white is usually accompanied by an effort to record the tones in their proper relation to one another. This is one kind of normal reproduction. 1. *Contrasty reproduction* is pictorial reproduction that departs from normal reproduction in such a way that the contrast of the observed image is excessive and objectionable. 2. *Flat reproduction* is pictorial reproduction that departs from normal reproduction in such a way that the CONTRAST of the observed image is insufficient and objectionable. 3. *Normal reproduction* is balanced, with dark and light proportionate to each other.

Re-recording: The electrical process of transferring sound records from one or more films or disks to other films or disks. Also the combining of all tracks (SOUND EFFECTS, DIALOGUE, music, etc.) onto one final release-track.

Resolution, Resolution Power: The ability of a LENS or emulsion to render fine detail in a photographic image.

Retake: A reshooting of a SCENE after the main PRODUCTION has finished filming/taping. It is an expensive process and is avoided when possible. On many filming assignments *video* replays often avoid the problem of retakes, as any given TAKE can be played back immediately.

Reveal Shot: A SHOT that widens out and opens up by pulling or zooming back to show where we are, often with an element of surprise.

Reversal Film: A film which, after EXPOSURE, is PROCESSED to produce a POSITIVE image on the same film rather than the customary NEGATIVE image. If exposure is made by printing from a negative, a negative image is produced directly.

Reversal Optical: A method of reversing the direction of motion of a SHOT by turning it over and rephotographing it in an optical printer, so that the emulsion side becomes the BASE side and vice versa.

Reverse: The opposite angle of a single or group-angled shot. If the camera is filming over the POINT OF VIEW of A, and looking at B, the reverse would be from the point of view of B looking at A.

Reverse Action: Action that goes backward on a TV or movie screen. In filming, this is done by shooting with the camera upside down, then turning the processed film end-over-end.

Revolving Stage: A playing-area STAGE that turns on a heavy axle, moving the entire SCENE so that it disappears behind theatrical curtains, or into darkness, or merely refocuses its physical emphasis. Used originally in live theater and then movie musicals; now also in TV and MIXED MEDIA.

Rewinds: Geared rewinding devices on which a REEL or FLANGE may be mounted and rotated rapidly by hand or an electric motor. Used mainly in CUTTING ROOMS and projection rooms.

Ribbon Mike: A name for a high-sensitivity microphone developed in the late 30's and early 40's for radio. Still used for special recording sessions, especially for voice-over, where the sound of the actor or actress must be resonant, close and intimate.

Rigging: 1. Placing and linking up power lines to studio lights, generally based on a LIGHT PLOT. 2. Setting up special camera mounts, mechanical SPECIAL EFFECTS, sound baffles, PRACTICAL PROPS, supports and platforms.

Riser: A low platform a few inches in height for raising a light, a prop, an actor or a cameraman above the studio floor.

Roll: Noun: 1. A package of motion picture film as it is ordered and comes from the manufacturer. 2. A designation on a SLATE and corresponding production reports, such as "Roll #2, Scene #3." Indicates the film rolls as marked and/or the sequence in which they are used. 3. The exposed film to be developed as it goes into and comes out of the lab. Verb: Often a command. As in "Stand by . . . and roll!" A command to start the camera(s) turning, followed by acknowledgment(s) of "SPEED!" and the command "ACTION!" In documentary filming, the "roll" signal is often the only one given to the CAMERAMAN by the DIRECTOR or his assistant. This command is frequently a hand or visual signal rather than a vocal command. Sometimes this is because of great distances between the camera and director or because the director does not want the sound of his command to interfere with a speech being given, a song being sung, or any event where any extraneous sound would be interruptive.

Roller Stand: A century reflector mounted on a CENTURY STAND or on a general-utility stand, and on rollers, to give it easier mobility as it is utilized in a studio or a location shooting area.

Room Tone: A recording of sound presence, particularly in an INTERIOR situation or in a recording studio, where each environment has its own ambient sound.

Rotoscope: A mechanism for projecting single FRAMES of FILM. This allows them to be rephotographed for SPECIAL EFFECTS or for ANIMATION tracing.

Rough Cut: The version of the WORKPRINT of a film that follows ASSEMBLY in the film's progress toward completion. A form of PRESENCE.

Rushes: Prints rushed through the LAB, usually the day after the NEGATIVE has been exposed. Rushes may be picture, sound or COMPOSITE. Also called DAILIES.

S

Safe-Action Area: Safety margin on the edges of the film allowing for TV cropping within the FRAME. Also called *TV cutoff*. Many cameras have optional or built-in TV cutoff plates for viewing and filming.

Safety Base: A slow-burning film BASE now used exclusively in professional motion picture production. At the present time this term is synonymous with ACETATE BASE.

SAG: The abbreviation for SCREEN ACTORS GUILD.

Salad: See JAM.

Sample Print: A COMPOSITE PRINT approved for release in which all corrections found necessary in previous trial-COMPOSITES have been incorporated. Also called *final trial composite*.

Sandbag: Standard working tool in film and TV. Its use developed out of live theater, where it served as a curtain-pull counterweight and as a support or augmenting weight for stage legs and braces to help hold up the scenery. In film it is also used to weigh down REFLECTOR stands or light stands on exterior shots, especially on windy days. It is used as ballast to smooth camera DOLLY moves and as an improvised ground-level camera-mount.

Saturation: The measurement of the purity and vividness of a color. Also the clarity of the hue. Vibrant, glowing color with optimum distinctness can be described as "fully saturated." It decreases in saturation as it moves nearer to a neutral gray.

Saturation Booking: Booking a film with necessary prints in a given area, augmented with a heavy ad campaign.

Scenario: See SCREENPLAY.

Scene: A subdivision of an *act* in live theater. In film, a scene is usually synonymous with a SHOT. Or a scene may be filmed with one basic number from end to end, then broken down for coverage into *scene numbers*, with each sequential number moving up. For example, a full dramatic scene may be composed of scene numbers 26–29 and slated and filmed as such in the MASTER SCENE. After that, 26, 27, 28, and 29 are filmed separately. These are generally COVERAGE shots. If the DIRECTOR wants to add an insert in, let us say, scene 27, it can be slated 27-A. In film—and tape—scene number and slate number are the same.

Scoop: A semicircular-shaped light trough powered by 500- to 1500-watt globes. A soft light.

Scoring: Composing, arranging, orchestrating, copying and recording the music. In LIBRARY scoring it is essentially a job of selecting CUES and laying them into the picture.

Scoring Session: A live-performance session for recording the musical score.

Scratched Print: A print that has been deliberately scratched, usually in a mutilator, to prevent its unauthorized duplication. Scratched prints are normally supplied by stock-shot libraries for viewing purposes.

Scratch Track: A roughly recorded SOUND TRACK made IN SYNCH to the picture, to be used as a guide in editorial synchronization or for FOLEYING and SCORING SESSIONS. (See also SYNCHRONISM, SYNCH SOUND)

Screen: In film, the projected photographic image is formed on a whitish screen, which may have a matte, beaded or metallic surface, and is often perforated in order to transmit sound freely from loudspeakers mounted behind the screen.

Screen Brightness: Full range of luminance emitted by a SCREEN. Measured in candles per square foot.

Screen Direction: The particular direction, left or right, as seen by the audience, in which the ACTOR is looking or moving. This is also sometimes referred to as *frame direction* and *camera direction*. MASTER SCENES and COVERAGE should all be congruent in screen direction.

Screenplay: Working SCRIPT for the film, evolving from concept to outline to rough treatment to SHOOTING SCRIPT.

Screen Test: Originally a test made of an ACTOR or actors doing a specially selected scene. The scene could be a specific one if the scene test was for a particular film, or a general one, even one selected by the actor(s), if the screen test was to determine whether the actors were to be signed to studio contract. As most contract players were dropped from the studios, and screen tests became more expensive, the filming of such tests came to an end, with some rare exceptions. Today, tests are made on tape. Auditions for TV shows and especially TV commercials are also taped to show to the client at another time or to send to a different city for client viewing.

Scribe: Tool used by editors to scratch the emulsion. This is done with the sharply pointed scribe in order to conform the original footing for SPLICING.

Scrim: Light diffuser set in front of a LIGHTING source to soften or "thin out" the light. A scrim can be a wire-mesh one set in a metal frame, or spun glass, parachute material, translucent plastic materials, etc. A wire-mesh unit is put in as a *single*, that is, one scrim. When a second one is added it is referred to as a *double*. If a FLAG is made of translucent material, it is called a scrim. Its effect is partly to cut off, partly to diffuse, the source of light near which it is placed; it is thus midway between a GOBO and a DIFFUSER. On the legitimate stage a scrim is a diaphanous curtain of gauze or similar materials that can be front-lit to be opaque or back-lit to give a diffuse lighting and lend a sense of fantasy or unreality to the performers onstage. In film and VIDEOTAPE lighting, the scrim is placed in front of the lights to soften the glare and/or to reduce overall light level.

Script: A written prescription for the making of any film. In its early stages it is often designated a TREATMENT; in its final stages, as a SHOOTING SCRIPT. (See also SCREENPLAY)

Script Clerk: The person responsible on a SET or on LOCATION for keeping a record of all SCENES and TAKES, recording technical notes on them and presenting this information in a useful form for the CUTTER. Also responsible for information for RETAKES of the same scene at a different time. Also called *script supervisor.*

SEG: The abbreviation for SCREEN EXTRAS GUILD.

Segue: Used in radio as a script direction, indicating a piece of transition music from one scene to another. Also sometimes used in TV scripts; rarely in screenplays (See also BRIDGE, STING)

Senior: Also called a 5K. This is a large, focusable LAMP with a mounted FRESNEL LENS and powered by a 5000-watt globe. It is midway between a JUNIOR and a 10K.

Sequence: A section of a film that is more or less complete in itself and which sometimes begins and ends with a FADE. However, sequences frequently end with DISSOLVES or even CUTS, which give a better flow to the action than fades. In a comparison with writing, a SHOT may be taken as equal to a sentence; a scene, a paragraph; a sequence, a chapter.

Set: An artificial construction that forms the scene of a tape or motion picture shot or series of shots.

Setup: 1. Physical placement of a camera in a specific spot, SET or locale. 2. The place itself to which the camera is moved: "Okay, that's it for here! Next setup."

Shooting Schedule: The breakdown in minutes, hours and days of the shooting time allocated by PAGE, SCENE or locale, of the production to be filmed/taped.

Shooting Script: The final working SCRIPT of a film. It details the shots one by one in relation to their accompanying DIALOGUE or other sound.

Shot: An elemental division of a film into sections. In commercial practice, a shot is more often called a SCENE, especially in referring to the SCRIPT. The common descriptions of shots are necessarily relative to the kind of picture of which they form a part. 1. A *close shot* (CLOSE-UP) is one taken with the camera close, or apparently close, to the subject, which is often a human face filling the field. Abbreviated CS or CU. 2. A *dolly shot* is one in which the camera moves bodily from one place to another on a special support such as a DOLLY or BOOM. Also called a *trucking shot*. 3. An *establishing shot* is a long shot, usually in EXTERIORS, which establishes the whereabouts of the scene. 4. A *high shot* is one that looks down on the subject from a height. 5. An *insert shot* is a shot of some objects relating to the scene, which is CUT into a SEQUENCE to help explain the action. 6. A *long shot* is one in which the object of principal interest is, or appears to be, far removed from the camera. Abbreviated LS. 7. A *low shot* is one that looks up at the subject, often from the ground level. 8. A *medium-close shot* is intermediate in distance between a close shot and a medium shot. Abbreviated MCS. 9. A *medium-long shot* is one intermediate in distance between a medium shot and a long shot. Abbreviated MLS. 10. A *medium shot* (*mid shot*) is one that shows a person at full height or views a scene at normal viewing distance. Abbreviated MS. 11. A *moving shot* is a shot made from some moving object such as an airplane or an automobile. 12. A *pan shot* is one in which the camera PANS across the screen. 13. A *reaction shot* is a shot inserted in a DIALOGUE sequence to show the effect of an actor's words on others in the scene, usually in close-up. More generally, any shot focusing on reactions. 14. A *two-shot* is a shot containing two characters, as a rule close to the camera. The term *three-shot* has a corresponding meaning. 15. A *zoom shot* is one taken with a ZOOM LENS. Verb: To film or tape a production; derived from cameramen's argot: "He shot the last scene yesterday." "How many films have you shot?"

Shrinkage: Film mass loss caused by rapid reduction in moisture right after PROCESSING or incremental shrinking over a long period of time.

Shutter: Device that momentarily covers the camera's aperture during the fraction of a second in which the film is moved between EXPOSURES.

Sight Gag: An action joke; fully or primarily visual. Not basically relying on verbal elements. A silent-comedy bit.

Single: 1. A shot of one person. 2. See under SCRIM.

Single-Card: An unshared screen CREDIT, the only one in a FRAME. Photographed on a single titling-card.

Single System: A method of sound recording in which the sound is originally recorded on the same strip of film as the picture image. Owing to difficulties in cutting caused by the difference between camera and editorial SYNCHRONISM, and to sensitometric disadvantages, single-system sound has been almost wholly abandoned in favor of double-system sound recording except for news coverage and some DOCUMENTARY interviews.

Sixteen mm (16mm): Used primarily for filming DOCUMENTARIES; tape is replacing film in TV news departments. Also used for low-budget commercials. Even FEATURE-LENGTH films are shot in 16mm and blown up to 35mm.

Skipping Effect: See STROBING.

Slate Board: A board placed in front of the camera at the beginning or end of each TAKE or each SCENE, which identifies the scene and the take and gives the name of the picture, the DIRECTOR, and the CAMERAMAN. (See also CLAPPER BOARD)

Slates: See SLATE BOARD.

Slow Motion: Motion of the film in the camera faster than the standard rate, which therefore results in the action appearing slower than normal when the film is projected at the standard rate.

Slug: A piece of LEADER inserted into a picture or sound WORKPRINT to replace damaged or missing footage.

SMPTE: The abbreviation for SOCIETY OF MOTION PICTURE AND TELEVISION ENGINEERS.

Soap Opera: Originally a daytime serial on radio that developed in New York and Chicago in the 30's. Since many of these serials had soap products sponsoring them, they came to be known as soap operas. The name stuck when the daytime serials re-emerged on TV, and when they moved to prime time.

Society of Motion Picture and Television Engineers: Group of sound, camera and LAB technicians who run seminars, publish books and scientific papers, and encourage the maintenance of high technical standards in TV and film.

Sodium Process: One way of making a traveling MATTE. The action is filmed in front of a yellow screen lit by sodium-vapor lamps.

Soft-Edge Wipe: A kind of WIPE in which the boundary line between the two SHOTS is softened or blurred, often by shooting the wipe masks out of focus. The degree of softness can be controlled.

Software/Hardware: Programs produced for or transferred to VIDEOTAPES are called software. Software is played on equipment designed to handle its particular format: $\frac{1}{2}''$, $\frac{3}{4}''$, $1''$. This equipment for recording, copying and playing the tapes is called hardware.

Sound Camera: A camera designed for sound shooting (i.e., picture and sound) and therefore silenced so as not to produce camera noise. The term is also applied to the recording camera in which the sound image is transferred to film via a modulator and a modulated beam of light or its magnetic equivalent.

Sound Dissolve: Analogous to picture DISSOLVE. A brief overlap of two SOUND TRACKS.

Sound Effects: All sounds, other than synchronized voices, NARRATION and music, which may be recorded on the SOUND TRACK of a film. Prior to RE-RECORDING, these effects usually occupy a separate sound track or tracks called sound effects track(s). Often abbreviated FX.

Sound Effects Library: An indexed or catalogued collection of the most commonly used SOUND EFFECTS that may be required by the editing department of a studio. Sound effects are most conveniently recorded on film, but are often re-recorded (see RE-RECORDING) from disks and from unperforated magnetic tape.

Sound Reader: Instrument for SOUND TRACK PLAYBACKS, used in editing.

Sound Speed: Internationally standardized speed of 24 FRAMES per second, for cameras and projectors, for synchronous picture and sound.

Sound Stripe: A thin band of iron oxide applied to the edge of a strip of film.

Sound Track: A narrow band, along one side of a sound film, which carries the sound record. In some cases several such bands may be used, such as in stereophonic recording, and sometimes for foreign release, where the music and EFFECTS will be kept but the voices dubbed (see DUBBING). *Multiple sound tracks* are used in stereophonic recording, that is, a group of sound tracks separate from one another but on one piece of film.

Sound Truck: A mobile conveyance fitted up with a sound recording channel. It usually carries drums on which microphone and other cables are wound.

Soup: Lab argot for chemical developing solutions.

Special Effects: A generic term for trick effects that are artificially constructed, as a rule in a studio separate from the main shooting stages. Special effects include split screens, matting, models and combination FOREGROUNDS and BACKGROUNDS.

Speed: 1. Speed is a generic term for the magnitude of light transmission of some part of a photographic system, usually an emulsion or a LENS. *Emulsion speed* is the sensitivity of a photographic emulsion to light. *Lens speed* is the light-admitting index of a lens, usually measured by its F or T number. 2. The correct speed at which a film mechanism is designed to run. The cry "Speed!" means that a sound or picture camera has reached synchronous speed. It is the signal for the director to call "Action!"

Spider: A device of three pieces of metal spreading out approximately 120° apart from a central core. There is a cuplike indentation at the ends of the pieces, and a clamping device. This allows tripod legs to be positioned and secured. The pieces are adjustable so that they can be spread. Hence the spider is also referred to as a *spreader*. The function of the spider is to stop TRIPOD legs from slipping on smooth surfaces, and to keep tripod-leg points from gouging into wood, marble or carpeting.

Splice, Splicing: The joining together of two pieces of film end to end so that they form one continuous piece of film is called splicing, and the joint is called a splice. Splices are of two kinds: *butt splices* and *lap splices*. 1. A *butt splice* is created when the ends of two pieces of film are made to abut against each other. This technique is seldom used except for the cutting of picture-release negatives, when it is important to retain frames that would be lost in a lap splice. 2. A *lap splice* occurs when the ends of two pieces of film are made to overlap. They may be united by applying film cement to the overlapped area after removing any emulsion present. A *negative splice* is a narrower type of lap splice used for splicing NEGATIVE and POSITIVE original picture material in order to make the printed-through image of the splice invisible (or, in 16mm, as little visible as possible) under all normal projection conditions. A *positive splice* is a wider type of lap splice, often used by film exchanges in the repair of RELEASE PRINTS.

Splicer: A machine needed to SPLICE two lengths of film together. Splicers are often classed as *hot* or *cold*, according to whether heat is or is not applied to the film joint to hasten the drying of the cement.

Split Reels: Standard REELS having one removable side, so that a CORE may be mounted on the spindle and wound film taken off at will and transferred to a FLANGE or a can without having to undergo rewinding.

Spotting: The process whereby the location of individual words or modulations on a SOUND TRACK can be accurately determined. This is accomplished with a sound MOVIOLA.

Spreader: See SPIDER.

Sprocket: A wheel carrying regularly spaced teeth of the correct pitch and separation to engage with film perforations and to move the film forward or in reverse while maintaining proper SYNCHRONISM, and, where necessary, REGISTRATION.

Squeeze Ratio: Horizontal compression in an anamorphic image, relative to its height.

Staff: For purposes of BUDGET and logistical planning, the staff is regarded as everyone but the performers. The CREW is regarded as *operational staff* and the others as PRODUCTION STAFF, although these categories often overlap. An example of production staff would be all those working on a given shooting assignment who work directly for the studio or production company: PRODUCER, line producer, PRODUCTION MANAGER, production associate, DIRECTOR (in some cases), production secretary and others. Those hired by their function are considered operational staff: CAMERAMEN, GRIP, soundmen, STUNTPERSONS, drivers and others. Sometimes these categories are simply referred to as production staff and/or crew.

Stage: The floor of a studio on which shooting takes place is called a stage, or soundstage when used for sound shooting.

Staging: Full blending of settings, wardrobe, LIGHTING, costumes, CAST and action for filming/taping.

Standby: A direction or signal to alert CREW and performers to prepare for the next immediate SCENE or SHOT.

Standby Light: A light, usually orange or red, alerting an actor or announcer that the next CUE is immediately upcoming. The "on" light is red. A radio term, sometimes used in TV and film.

Stand-in: Performer who is assigned to "stand in" for the STAR. The stand-in is usually of the same sex, basic height and body build, so that he or she can be used when the star's acting area needs to be lighted or when there is a LONG SHOT of the back of the star riding away in a car, or when a given action by the star verges on stuntwork. Sometimes a stand-in is also a STUNTPERSON.

Star: Leading player who is well known and constantly publicized. The star has billing above the FEATURE PLAYERS, and sometimes enjoys lettering bigger than the name of the DIRECTOR or PRODUCER, depending on the status of the star at the time of the film: is he or she on the way up or down, or making a comeback? How bankable is the name?

Star Filter: Special FILTER that makes star-shaped HIGHLIGHT reflections. Used to give special visual emphasis, often to glamorize or romanticize a SCENE or a product. Used a great deal in the late 60's to mid-70's. Still used today, but more sparingly.

Starlet: Originally meaning "little STAR," and used for feminine contract players or rising INGENUES. Today it refers to new female faces who have become TV or film regulars.

Start Marks: A sync mark on one or more film tracks designating the point from which an operation such as printing, projection or synchronizing is to begin. ACADEMY LEADERS incorporate two start marks, one for picture and one for sound.

Stat: A reverse-printing card: black for white, white for black, used for titling (see TITLE) and CREDITS.

Steadicam: Trade name for a body-braced self-balancing rig on which a camera can be mounted, allowing the cameraman to walk through crowds, into an elevator and out again, upstairs or downstairs, etc., with maximum fluidity and minimal jolt. Panaglide is the Panavision counterpart to the Steadicam.

Step-Optical Printer: LAB printer that exposes (see EXPOSURE) a specified film segment a FRAME at a time.

Stet: Term taken from journalism and typesetting. From the Latin, it means "let it stand." For example, a half-page of dialogue may be crossed out, then reinstated. To indicate the reinstatement, "stet" is written alongside the deleted material.

Still: A photograph taken with a still camera or a still shot blown up from a motion picture frame.

Still Man: Professional still photographer assigned to a PRODUCTION, to take SHOTS of CAST, CREW, SETS and general production activity.These photos are used for publicity purposes and a production record.

Sting: A musical chord, generally loud and staccato, within a SCENE as dramatic punctuation or as a SEGUE to the next scene.

Stock Footage: The material in a FILM LIBRARY consisting of SHOTS such as geographical ESTABLISHING SHOTS, historical material, and footage of other general application that is likely to be used on many productions over a period of time, and is consequently kept in stock for general use. These shots are of important events, famous places, and whatever it would be impracticable to shoot for each production.

Stop: A fixed APERTURE designed to limit the amount of light passing through a LENS. Also applied to any specific setting of a movable LENS DIAPHRAGM, which designates the effective speed of a lens working at other than its full aperture. (See also LENS, APERTURE)

Stopping Down: The process of reducing the APERTURE of a LENS by means of a stop or diaphragm. (See also LENS, APERTURE and LENS DIAPHRAGM)

Story Board: Sometimes used in film preparation, when convenient to make sketches of key incidents in the action. These are then arranged in order on a board called a story board and captioned.

Straight Man: The performer who feeds the straight lines to the comic, so that the comic can deliver the gag line or punch line.

Strike: To take down all the SETS, electrical gear and special scenic or technical devices that have been specially rigged for a given shooting session (after filming/taping). "Okay, strike this set!"

Strobing: A SCREEN image—or part of an image—distractingly fractionated by its jerking motion. This is especially noticeable in perpendicular lines moving by the camera, for example, panning a white picket fence or a group of close-set architectural columns. Also the deliberately produced effect of this movement, with a ghosting and trailing pattern following the direction of the action.

Stuntperson: A performer who does the dangerous falls, leaps, car chases, fast and trick horseback riding, fights, etc., for the STARS or principal ACTORS. A stuntperson is often chosen for his/her physical resemblance—at least at a distance—to the actor being doubled. Replacing the term *stuntman*.

Subbing Layer: An adhesive coating that holds the film emulsion to its BASE.

Subjective Camera: The viewpoint of camera-as-actor: you are seeing the scene through the eyes of one of the principal actors. A hand-held POINT-OF-VIEW shot moving through a crowd is an example. Or a fist coming into the lens when the camera represents the movements of one of the fighters; you, the spectator, receive the punch. Used to intensify audience involvement in a scene. Attempts to carry a full-length feature entirely with subjective camera have not been successful.

Subject-to-Camera: The actual distance of the leading person or object in the scene to the camera itself. The camera point is often measured to the spot where the film is actually exposed as it goes through the camera.

Subliminal Cut: A cut of a few FRAMES, a fraction of a second. Used to foreshadow or intensify mood or to give a sense of freneticism, violence or imbalance to a scene.

Substandard: A term used to describe all gauges or widths of film smaller than the theater standard of 35mm, the most important being 16mm.

Subtext: The real "message" beneath the veneer of words. The nonverbal matrix of what a scene is all about. The good actor and director use text as a guide to the root of the scene—the subtext.

Subtitle: A translation of the DIALOGUE into lettering in the lower third of the SCREEN.

Sungun: A small, intense, hand-held, battery-powered light. This hot portable unit throws strong light in its immediate area, and is used often in TV news coverage and DOCUMENTARY filmings.

Supered Titles (Superimposed Titles): TITLES over stationary or moving backgrounds.

Super-16: 16mm film in which the SOUND TRACK area is used to add extended width to the FRAME ratio. This gives a larger image, and one that is in wide-screen ratio. Used for low-budget features, DOCUMENTARIES and short subjects, and often blown up to 35mm master for theatrical use.

Sweephand: The large hand on a stopwatch that clocks off the seconds or fractions of seconds. Used for timing DIALOGUE, action, music cues, or EFFECTS.

Sweetening: The adding of additional instruments to a music track that has already been recorded, either live or by RE-RECORDING two recordings into one COMPOSITE.

Swish Pan: A type of panning SHOT in which the camera is swung very rapidly on its vertical axis, the resulting film producing a blurred sensation when viewed.

Switcher: In TV, the control-room technician in charge of electronically switching from one camera to another.

Synch Mark: An editor's scratch mark, grease-pencil indication or punched hole to indicate the start frame of the picture track and/or the SOUND TRACK.

Synchronism: The relation between picture and sound films with respect either to the physical location on the film or films or to the time at which corresponding picture and sound are seen and heard. One speaks of picture and sound as being IN SYNC.

Synchronizer: A device used in CUTTING ROOMS for maintaining SYNCHRONISM between film tracks. It consists of two or more SPROCKETS rigidly mounted on a revolving shaft. The tracks are placed on the sprockets and accurately positioned by their perforations so that they can be wound along by REWINDS while maintaining a proper synchronous relationship.

Sync Pop: Sound signal of one FRAME at the front end of SOUND TRACKS to ensure alignment with the picture.

Sync Sound: Sound that matches FRAME-to-frame with the picture, especially critical in lip movements as ACTORS speak DIALOGUE in CLOSE SHOTS. The frame-to-frame marriage of sound and picture.

Synopsis: 1. A short or preliminary version of the SCRIPT of a film. 2. A summary of a complete film, often intended to catalogue its contents for a FILM LIBRARY.

T

Tail: End of a film. When wound with end on the outside of the film roll it is often marked *tails out*.

Take: Each performance of a piece of action in front of a live camera is called a take, the successive takes usually being numbered from 1 upward. These take numbers are recorded by photographing a numbered SLATE BOARD and noted by the SCRIPT CLERK, and on camera and sound reports.

Take-up Reel: The REEL on which film is wound after being run on film machinery such as projectors, cameras or printers.

Take-up Spool: A plastic notched spool used in filming to take up film fed through the camera mechanism. A spool also serves as a CORE for the film ROLL itself. These spools are also used, in conjunction with FLANGES and split REELS, in editing (see EDIT) the film.

Talent: As opposed to CREW, any person or animal working as an on-camera performer.

Talkie: Colloquial name from the late 20's from a "talking motion picture": a picture with sound.

Talking Head: A description of a style of reportage or DOCUMENTARY filming in which the main themes and structural lines are carried by on-camera interviewees talking straight into the camera, as opposed to re-created events or CINÉMA VERITÉ.

Tape Splice: Film SPLICE made with a BUTT SPLICER and short bit of splicing tape.

TD: The abbreviation for TECHNICAL DIRECTOR.

Teaser: An introduction to an episode or special (radio or TV) that catches the attention of the audience in order to hold it through the COMMERCIAL BREAKS and carry it into and hold it through the entire program.

Tea Wagon: Colloquial term for a small, wheeled console sometimes used by MIXERS when controlling sound on a soundstage.

Technical Adviser: Person hired to give historical, technical or biographical information regarding the subject, personal or general, of a motion picture or TV special. For example, a retired star might act as a technical adviser on a biography about himself or herself, or an expert on American history might advise on a film about the Civil War.

Technical Director (TD): In TV this is often the floorman. He or she cues actors and sometimes cameras and sees to it that all equipment is functioning properly. In film the TD coordinates the efforts of the various tech crews: for example, sound with camera, SPECIAL EFFECTS with GRIPS.

Technicolor: One of the major world-class film laboratories. One of the leading pioneers in color cinematography. The Technicolor 3-strip process is considered by many to have been the ultimate in achieving beauty of color, and in separation and delineation. It was abandoned by the studios because it was too expensive to utilize in FEATURE-LENGTH production. The process is now being used, however, in the Orient.

Telephoto Lens: A LENS, usually of greater than normal FOCAL LENGTH, so constructed that the back FOCUS is different from the effective focal length of the lens: usually less, in order to increase compactness; sometimes more, in order to allow for the use of a WIDE-ANGLE LENS in a camera where a prism must be interposed between lens and film. More generally, this term is mistakenly used to designate a long-focus lens (See also LONG-FOCUS LENS under LENS)

That's a Buy: Meaning, in TV, "That's an acceptable TAKE. Mark it OK." Or, in film, "That's a print."

Theme: The underlying statement in a dramatic work, or motif or melody in a musical score.

Theme Song: Title song for a TV series or a motion picture. The identifying musical "logo" of a TV program.

Thirty-Five mm (35mm): For years, the standard feature motion picture FILM-STOCK size. It is still the basic stock for FEATURE-LENGTH films and high-budget commercials. For features, however, it is sometimes replaced by wide-gauge film (65 or 70mm), or by 16mm, which is then blown up to 35mm.

Threading: The act of placing film on the proper SPROCKETS and rollers, aligning it in the GATES and forming LOOPS, and doing whatever else is necessary to ensure its proper passage through a camera, PROJECTOR, VIEWER or printer.

Throw: Effective distance for holding a projected image clearly on the screen. The efficiency of the throw depends upon both or either projector and film image.

Tilting: Pivotal vertical movement of the camera, contrasted with *panning* (see PAN).

Time: Evaluation of proper printer-light setting appropriate to a specific SHOT.

Time-Footage Computer: A footage-to-time wheel, accurately correlating these factors for both 16mm and 35mm. Copyrighted by ASC cameraman Alan Stensvold in 1944.

Time Lapse: A specific length of time between the exposure of each individual frame. Achieved by shooting, on a locked-down camera, one FRAME every few seconds, minutes, or other preset time frame. By using this technique, flowers grow rapidly before the eyes of film or TV audiences, clouds rush by at incredible speed, and traffic passes in a hectic, accelerated blur.

Timer: Person who makes the timing evaluations of each SHOT and decides how much, if any, color correction is necessary.

Timing Card: Guide list giving printer-light numbers, often SCENE by scene or even within-scene, for making prints from the original. The card is held for reference for making additional prints.

Title: 1. Any written material that appears on a film and is not a part of an original SCENE. 2. Registered name of the SCREENPLAY or teleplay. The person in whose name it is registered, or to whom it is transferred by sale, lease or power of attorney, is said to "have title" to the script. 3. *Credit titles* list the actors in a film and the technicians who made it. 4. *Creeper titles* are often used to carry the names of the CAST of a film. They "creep" slowly around on a large, unseen drum in front of the camera. Sometimes called *roll-up titles*.

Title Song: A song for a movie, TV special or series that includes the title of the show in its lyrics or describes what the story is all about, as in the ballad in the classic film *High Noon*.

Top Billing: First and/or most prominent CREDITS on the screen, mostly a negotiable item in STAR contracts, but also for PRODUCERS, DIRECTORS, writers, CAMERAMEN and composers.

Traveling Shot: A shot in which the camera moves bodily in relation to its object. Same as DOLLYING shot.

Treatment: A more or less detailed preparation of a story and idea in film form, which has not yet been put into SCRIPT form.

Triangle: A device that is triangular or is shaped like a three-pointed star and which receives the three legs of a TRIPOD in order to prevent the legs from slipping apart. (See also SPIDER)

Tripod: A simple type of three-legged support, often used to hold FIELD CAMERAS as well as studio cameras.

Turret Lens: A revolving mount attached to the front of a camera, carrying three or more LENSES and enabling them in turn to be swung into position in front of the photographing APERTURE.

TV Cutoff: See SAFE-ACTION AREA.

TV Print: COMPOSITE color-film print that has been balanced for XENON projection.

Two-Shot: A SHOT that features two persons in the FOREGROUND.

Tyler Mount: The basic camera mount for use in helicopters and camera planes that fits inside the aircraft. It is a set of extended arms and counterweights which are adjustable to the size and the weight of the camera. The entire mount is ball-balanced on a small pivotal point to minimize vibration. There are also special custom-mounts that can be rigged outside the aircraft. To augment the flexibility of the exterior mounts, a video assist system is often used so the cameraman, and sometimes the director, can see what is being filmed.

U

UHF: The abbreviation for Ultrahigh Frequency.

Umbrella and Stand: A silverized photographer's reflecting umbrella for bouncing light into the scene and, indirectly, onto the actors or set pieces. Often used in TV commercials for photographing the sponsor's product.

Undercrank: The term originated in the silent film days, when cameras were hand-cranked. To run the camera slower than sound speed (24 FPS), resulting in speeded-up action when the developed image is projected.

Underwater Housing: A waterproof casing in which a camera can be inserted and totally enclosed, but still be operated outside this casing for underwater filming.

Union: A workmen's organization. A guild. The craftsmen and artists working at the major studios are nearly all union members. In independent, off-the-lot film and tape productions the employees are often a mix of union and nonunion. The unions are supported primarily or solely by membership dues. The function of these unions/guilds is to set up working rules, adjust base rates, arrange for membership meetings and social functions, call strikes, issue bulletins, and in some cases offer legal advice and apprenticeship/intern openings for those starting in the particular discipline of the union.

Union Card: Card issued to UNION members to show their active status. It is supposed to be on the person of any union member when working on a production or on salary at a studio or production company.

Union List: A list put out by the UNION to its membership of signatory and fair-practice production companies. Also a list of nonsignatories and/or companies whose labor practices the union deems unfair. Union list also means a list of those members who are on active status and available for employment.

Unit Manager: The person in business control of a production unit on LOCATION.

Unit Production Manager (UPM): PRODUCTION MANAGER assigned to a specific filming/taping group or production. A LOCATION MANAGER.

Up: A multipurpose word with various uses depending on the context. If an actor or actress has the lines down cold and comes in quickly on CUE, that person is "up in his or her lines" and knows them well. However, if the performer begins a TAKE, suddenly goes blank, and with a glazed stare says, "Sorry, I'm up," he or she has momentarily forgotten the lines. To say that an actor or actress is "really up in performance" means that the person is working with full technical and creative involvement in a scene; at peak capacity.

Up and Under: A music or SOUND EFFECTS term that originated in radio and is sometimes used in SCREENPLAYS and teleplays. It means that the music or sound that has already been established as a PRESENCE behind the SCENE, now rises in volume and then drops back under to a BACKGROUND presence, allowing other sound to have FOREGROUND prominence. For example: The scene is an office building. Both music-of-the-city and traffic sounds are heard behind the DIALOGUE of the actors. The scene switches to outside the office in the busy street below. The music and street noises come up to full strength, the scene switches to back inside the office, and once again traffic sounds and music drop to a background presence. The dialogue is highlighted *up and out*, meaning that the sound and/or music rises in volume and then drops out completely.

V

Variable-Area Recording: Recording by means of an OPTICAL-SOUND RECORDER designed to produce a SOUND TRACK divided laterally into opaque and transparent areas.

Variable-Density Recording: Recording by means of an OPTICAL-SOUND RECORDER designed to produce a number of density gradations perpendicular to the edge of the SOUND TRACK and extending across its full width. The distance between gradations is determined by the recorded frequency.

VCR: See VIDEOCASSETTE RECORDER.

Velocilator: A movable camera mount intermediate in size between a DOLLY and a BOOM. It will carry a heavy camera up to a height of about six feet, but it is not intended to be raised or lowered rapidly while the camera is running. The movement is usually hand operated.

VHF: The abbreviation for *very high frequency*.

VHM: A $\frac{1}{2}''$ home tape-recording format. The Beta system.

Video: 1. A common name for television, especially when referring to it technically. 2. A designation on a two-column SCRIPT to indicate sound: for example, to distinguish AUDIO from the picture (the video).

Video Assist: A small videotaping camera, recorder and PLAYBACK system that records filmed TAKES directly through the film camera and sound units, with the capability of playing back any take immediately after it is completed. This allows the DIRECTOR, PRODUCER and client to view and evaluate the take before deciding whether to move on to the next scene or to first go for another take. Also called *video playback*.

Videocassette Recorder: Any VIDEOTAPE recorder that both records and/or plays back a tape in any of the formats: $1/2''$, $3/4''$ or $1''$. The $1/2''$ in America is the Beta system; the $3/4''$ is the U-Matic system. These formats are for both professional and/or home use. The $1''$ system, however, is used almost exclusively for professional VIDEO recording, replacing the standard $2''$ tapes used originally for television broadcasting. Also, the $1''$ system does not operate with self-contained cassettes but with recording tape moving from feed roll to take-up roll.

Videodisk: A disk or "record" on or in which are stored the images to be electronically reassembled for VIDEO transmission. The CED–RCA system is a needle-in-groove system, similar to the udio records, the old phonograph system. MCA–Universal developed the LV (Laser Video) system, which was taken over by IBM and then by Pioneer. The system is played by a light beam with no pickup device actually touching the disk. These are the two basic American systems. In Japan the VHD system utilizes a magnetic field with a "needle" floating over it but never touching the disk.

Video Format: There are three basic VIDEO-broadcasting formats in the world. In the United States and Japan it is the NTSC format, with 525 lines. The SECAM system, used in Russia and France, and the PAL system, used throughout the rest of Europe and in Australia, both use over 600-line images.

Videotape: A tape for recording and playing back a VIDEO scene. The general term *tape* can refer to a videotape or to an AUDIO tape only; the direct meaning to be determined by context.

Viewer: A simple film-viewing device without the complications of a MOVIOLA. The film can be moved at any desired speed through it. It is usually mounted between two REWINDS.

Viewfinder: An optical device forming part of a camera or attached to it, which provides an image (usually magnified) approximating that which is formed by the LENS on the film. 1. A *direct viewfinder* is a type that usually incorporates a FOCUSING MICROSCOPE which enables the cameraman to scrutinize the image which the lens is actually forming on the film. It therefore requires no correction for PARALLAX. 2. A *monitoring viewfinder* is one external to the camera and often to the BLIMP. It enables the cameraman to watch his or her scene while the camera is turning. It is usually equipped with accurate compensation for parallax, and in some designs gearing is provided to couple the finder to the lens-focusing mount. 3. A *reflex viewfinder* is a type of direct viewfinder used in some advance cameras which sees through the lens while the picture is being taken. It is constructed by means of a silvered mirror on the back of the SHUTTER which allows a continuous image to be formed for the eye (while the same is happening to the film) through PERSISTENCE OF VISION. The brightness of course varies with the lens APERTURE.

Viewing Restrictions: Limitations placed on screenings of leased or purchased EDUCATIONAL or INFORMATIONAL films: no paid admissions, no subcontracting for live, theatrical or television screenings, etc. The standard overall covering clause is "no direct optical projection for paying or nonpaying audiences."

Vignette: A short dramatic sketch. Some programs or films are made up of thematic vignettes, for example, the feature film *Twilight Zone*. Or a vignette may be part of a variety show featuring music, dance and drama.

Vignetting: A camera term for when something outside the LENS is cutting into the field of vision, for example, a LENS HOOD, a MATTE BOX or a LIGHTING GOBO, or when the lens is wider than the full APERTURE. The effect results in an extraneous image within the FRAME.

Visual Effects: A broad term that includes, and is sometimes synonymous with, SPECIAL EFFECTS. In its wide application it means not only special effects, but also SETS designed for light absorbency, pushed-stop filming (see PUSH), and customized LAB instructions, as well as special LIGHTING and creative utilization of standard camera FILTERS, SPEEDS and LENSES.

Visual Primary: A term meaning that the visual aspect of a film scene dominates the sound.

VTR: The abbreviation for VIDEOTAPE recorder.

VU Meter: Volume units meter used on many sound recorders and PLAYBACK units to register loud/soft gradations of amplitude.

W

Walla-Walla: A radio term meaning a general background burble of conversation. It comes from the observation that most of the subdued AD-LIBS coming from the actors off-mike sound as though they were chanting "Walla-Walla."

Warner Brothers: Early film studio dating from the "silent" days. On the verge of bankruptcy, Warner Brothers invested in a new sound process called Vitaphone. It supplied the SOUND TRACK for the first full-length talkie, *The Jazz Singer*. From this, Warners became one of the major studios, and remains so today.

Warning Bell: 1. In the projection room, a bell that rings a few moments before the end of a motion picture REEL to alert the projectionist that the next reel is coming up and to stand by the other projector to make the switchover. 2. On a soundstage, a loud bell that rings on the SET before a TAKE begins (one bell) to alert everyone to be quiet and to ready themselves for the take. Two bells means that the take is over—an all-clear signal.

Warning Light: Red blinking or rotating light outside a movie soundstage or TV stage to indicate filming or taping is under way and to be quiet and not to enter the stage until the light is switched off.

Whip: A sudden rapid move of the camera, for example, a SWISH PAN.

White Camera Tape: Differentiated from GAFFER'S TAPE or black/gray friction tape. Used mainly to put around the circumference of film cans to keep the cans together and to prevent light leaks. Also used to label the cans with marking pens and for laying on SLATE BOARDS for marking scene information.

Wide-Angle Lens: A LENS allowing a framed view of 60° or more. Used to photograph the panoramic or to include as much of a scene as possible in cramped quarters. In brief, to give a broader playing area to a given scene.

"Wild" Recording: Any sound recording that is not made synchronously with a picture record is called "wild" recording. SOUND EFFECTS and random voices are usually recorded this way; sometimes NARRATION and music. Also called *non-synch*.

Winds: FILM STOCK for loading into a camera is wound emulsion side *in*. This is called a *B-wind*. Double perforated stock for filming is wound the same way. *A-wind* stock is rarely used in filming, but is wound in this manner—emulsion side up, and with the single sprocket on the opposite side of the film roll—for printing.

Wipe: An optical effect between two succeeding SHOTS on the SCREEN in which the second shot appears and wipes the first off the screen along a visible line. The line may run from top to bottom, side to side, or in any one of a large number of patterns.

Woodshedding: Originally a musical term indicating "going to the woodshed and practicing on your instrument over and over until you get the sound you're after." It now also applies to actors, announcers and other performers, and means to go off alone to a place apart and practice music or rehearse DIALOGUE.

Workprint: A LAB print from developed ORIGINAL, used by the editor to first synch up to sound and then to put into a first ASSEMBLY. The visual material used for film editing.

Workprint, Picture: A POSITIVE print that usually consists of intercut daily prints (see INTERCUTTING and DAILIES), FILM LIBRARY prints, prints of DISSOLVES, MONTAGE, TITLES, etc., and has SYNCHRONISM constantly maintained with the corresponding sound WORKPRINT.

Workprint, Sound: A sound print that usually contains all of the tracks (original sound, DUBBED sound, SOUND EFFECTS, etc.), but often without the final musical score, which in most studios is added to the finished film.

Wrap: To end a shooting day. As a noun: "That's a wrap." As a verb: "Okay, let's wrap it!" At the end of filming: "That wraps the picture!"

X

X: A SLATE/SCENE identification. A letter, along with Y and Z, used to indicate general INSERT SHOTS that do not match any specific part of a numbered SCENE, and where an A, B or C lettering added to the scene, for example "Scene 72-A," would not be relevant. This might occur when a scene has already been slated "72-A," but while shooting this scene of a CUTAWAY REACTION SHOT, the director decides to pick up a shot of a day-by-day calendar on the desk. Since this shot might be used anywhere in the scene, or even in another scene, it would be marked and slated as 72-X. If an insert shot of a figurine next to the calendar is added immediately after that, as a directional afterthought, it would be slated 72-Y.

Xenon Projector: A motion picture theater PROJECTOR that is replacing the arc projector. Its advantages are that it uses a bulb instead of a burning carboniferous element, allowing a longer use of the projector before the bulb is changed and also not requiring a full venting system to carry off the extreme heat generated by an arc projector.

Xenon Tube: The common name for the bulb in the XENON PROJECTOR.

X-Fade: See CROSS-FADE.

X-Rated: One of four ratings given to films in RELEASE. G means "General," and indicates that the film is acceptable for all audiences, all ages: a family film. PG is an evaluation signifying "parental guidance," as some of the material might not be suitable for children. R means "restricted"; in this case, to those of a certain age. This age varies from sixteen to twenty-one, with eighteen being the Motion Picture Association of America's suggested age. X means that the material is for adults only—twenty-one and over. Often an X rating shows that the film deals with explicit sex.

Y

Y: A SLATE indication, with X and Z. (See X)

Yellow Filter Group: A series of FILTERS in the yellow range to intensify the yellow hues of a scene and warm it up.

Y Joint: An electrical connection of a main-trunk cable branching off into two cables, with connecting units at all three ends. Also called *Y cable*.

Yoke: A holding frame for LAMPS or REFLECTORS, mounted on a special stand, plate or clamp, or safety chained to an overhead grid support.

Yo-Yo: For the camera or microphone to PAN back and forth within a SCENE. Also called *ping-ponging*.

Z

Z: A SLATE indication, with X and Y. (See x)

Zoom: Real or apparent rapid motion of the camera toward its object is known as *zooming*. Pulling away from an object is called a *zoom-out*.

Zoom Lens: A LENS of variable magnification that enables zooming effects to be easily achieved without moving the camera toward its object. Parallactic effects (see PARALLAX), which usually accompany real movement, are of course absent from zoom lens shots, which are therefore most useful when the object is at a great distance, for example, a sports field. This lens has widespread use in television, where cameras often cannot move; for example, at conventions or football games.